HOME VIDEO
and the Changing Nature of the Television Audience

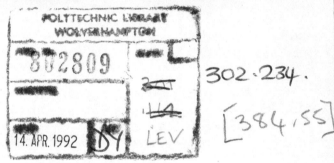
Mark R. Levy

University of Maryland

and

Barrie Gunter

Head of Research
Independent Broadcasting Authority

 John Libbey
LONDON · PARIS IBA

British Library Cataloguing in Publication Data
Levy, Mark R.
  Home video and the changing nature of
  the television audience. — (Television research monographs,
  ISSN 0951-3582;5).
  1. Society. Role of videotape recordings.
  I. Title   II. Gunter, Barrie   III. Series
  303.4′833

  ISBN 0-86196-175-7 (Hardback)
  ISBN 0-86196-188-9 (Paperback)

Published by
John Libbey & Company Ltd
80/84 Bondway, London SW8 1SF, England (01) 582 5266
John Libbey Eurotext Ltd
6 rue Blanche, 92120 Montrouge, France (1) 47 35 85 52

Typesetting in Century by E E Owens & Co Ltd., London SE15 4AZ
Printed in Great Britain by Whitstable Litho Ltd, Whitstable, Kent

CONTENTS

CHAPTER ONE

THE GROWTH OF HOME VIDEO

In not much more than a dozen years, the video cassette recorder has become a major part of the home communications environment. Indeed, from a world-wide perspective, no other new communication technology has reached such dramatic levels of home penetration (Communication Research Trends, 1985).

More than half of all Japanese households, for example, have video, while in some Arabian Gulf states, video penetration exceeds three-quarters of all television households (Boyd, 1987). And, while video penetration in Great Britain and the United States has not approached those levels, it has rapidly progressed to at least half of all television households. In short, the VCR has become nearly as commonplace as the television set to which it is attached.

Naturally enough, broadcasters have been intensely interested in the video phenomenon. This monograph attempts to inform that interest by providing an up-to-date assessment of video's impact in the United Kingdom. It is built around the findings of a major study of video use in Great Britain, designed by this volume's two authors and carried out under the auspices of the Research Department of the Independent Broadcasting Authority.

In the chapters which follow, specific aspects of video behaviour will be examined in detail. In this introductory chapter, we seek to place video research in a larger, theoretical context. The fundamental questions raised here – but scarcely resolved – are these: Does video represent something *significantly* new in the mass communication process? Is video a revolutionary or merely an evolutionary development? What are the most appropriate theoretical and conceptual tools for probing video behaviours?

Defining video

Video is more than microchips and iron oxides. It is a cultural artifact, subject to social and cultural definition. Ideas about what video is – and ought to be – come from the public, from the commercial sector, and from researchers. These ideas – some commonsensical, some scientific – are important for they are likely to influence how we use, study and make policy for video.

The public definition of video took on its current "shape" shortly after the introduction of home video in the mid-1970s. Advertisers and the public alike agreed that the VCR was a device first, to record television programmes for later replay ("time-shifting"); second, to build a home "library" of video-tapes; and third, to conveniently view hired or purchased tapes of movies, rock videos, or whatever (Buckwalter, 1978; Consumers Reports, 1980).

While this three-part "definition" of video has gained wide public acceptance, there are, however, more complex notions embedded in its commonplaceness. For example, do people "watch" video or do they watch television? In other words, does the audience consider video to be a unique form of communication, or merely part of the television set? Is video, as some (e.g. Baboulin et al, 1983) have suggested, an "unseen" device with little or no significance in itself. Or does the use of video in and of itself offer gratifications which make the technology intrinsically desirable and rewarding (Roe, 1983; Williams et al., 1985; Schoenbach and Hackforth, 1987). How, in a question partially examined in Chapter 2, do the perceived attributes of video compare with the gratifications offered by the "older" technologies of print and broadcast?

Some aspects of the public's definition of video become clearer after examining patterns of use. Several previous reports (e.g. Levy, 1983; Darkhow, 1985; Tydeman and Kelm, 1986; Wober, 1985) have concluded that video use in Western Europe and the United States is mostly for time-shifting purposes, largely complements existing patterns of television exposure and has only a negligible effect on broadcast viewing.

By contrast, video use in the Middle East or Third World, or by Third World nationals living in developed nations, appears to involve dramatically higher levels of pre-recorded cassette replays and little time-shifting (Media Development, 1985). Such cross-national differences in video use suggest that variations in media systems play an important, and so far largely unexplored part, in video behaviours.

Two other aspects of video behaviours – long-term patterns of video use (does time-shifting decline, for example, as the "novelty" of having a video wears off?) and "library-building" (how many tapes, for example, do people want and how many can they afford to collect?) – and their relationship to public definitions of videos have also been largely unstudied. We present some evidence about both in Chapters 5 and 6.

Video and social life

The impact of video on social life has been the subject of considerable speculation (see, for example, Baboulin *et al*, 1983; Gubern, 1985; Cubitt, 1986). Much of this speculation has focused either on the assumed deleterious consequences of video for social integration or the presumed salutary effect of video on cultural diversity.

What, for example, some scholars have asked, is the impact of video use on social cohesion? How does watching video affect social ties between members of, say, households, social classes, ethnic groups, or even nations? In Chapter 4, we examine the social context of video use as a first step towards answering some of those questions.

Similarly, the issue of cultural diversity–homogeneity also deserves investigation. Video's promoters have often held out the VCR as a means for substantially increasing the variety of media content available to audiences. However, one early study (Levy, 1980b) found that video households tended to time-shift programmes from a relatively limited number of genres (e.g. soap operas, sports, movies). Evidence from the UK, presented in several chapters in this monograph, tends to support that empirical finding.

Video and media effects

A substantial number of early studies of video have examined the impact of VCR use on children and adolescents (Barker, 1984; Barlow and Hill, 1985; Roe, 1985; Greenberg and Heeter, 1987). This research has focused primarily, although not exclusively, on the consequences of violent and pornographic materials when viewed on a video cassette recorder. Like much of the research on pornography and violence, these studies themselves have been the subject of considerable controversy and their interpretations and implications remain a matter of dispute.

While focusing on the effects of video content on children, little research has probed either the potential impact of other content on adults or effects associated with video exposure itself. Additional work is needed, for example, to gauge the effects on adult information-levels and behaviours which follow from exposure to "how-to-do-it" or hobby tapes, pre-recorded shopping catalogues, or compilations of news for special-ised audiences.

Further research is required, too, to determine first, whether the video user is a more active participant in the communication process (Levy, forthcoming); and second, whether that greater selectivity carries over into other media-related attitudes and behaviours. How, for example, does the ability to "fast-forward" through a video-recorded programme affect viewer attitudes toward the importance, "value", or enjoyment of those programmes and the commercial messages it contains (Yorke and Kitchen, 1985; Harvey and Rothe, 1986)?

Finally, given the worldwide availability of video, serious questions must be raised about the effects of "imported" programmes on audiences in Third World and developing nations. Simplistic charges of media imperialism and its alleged effects on individual and collective identities are not sufficient. Following the conceptual and methodological insights from recent encoding/decoding studies (see, for example, Morley, 1980; Liebes and Katz, 1986), it now becomes possible empirically to examine how videotape texts are "read" by audiences.

Overall, then, the task facing the broadcasting research community is clear. If video represents nothing less than a real change in the mass communication process, then we need to develop alternative frameworks, indeed alternative questions, for understanding it. If, however, as we suspect, the VCR phenomenon is largely evolutionary in nature, then video can be adequately studied using our existing, perhaps improved, research armoury. Either way, video is too important to ignore, but not yet well enough understood.

CHAPTER TWO

HOME VIDEO IN BRITAIN

The 1980s has been a decade of unprecedented expansion and development for mass media in the United Kingdom. Broadcast radio and television services have increased in number, while the established networks have extended their airtime. And within the home, a range of accessories and enhancements which can be used in conjunction with the television set – video recorders, video disc players, teletext and viewdata services, video games and personal computers – have become widely available. There are also alternative sources of programming to the broadcast services via cable and satellite.

The most significant development, perhaps, with the most direct impact and benefits for the average householder in the UK, has been the rapid penetration of home video recorders. Although the VCR had been around since the 1970s, it was not until 1980 that private ownership began to take off. Compared to 1979, when only negligible numbers of homes possessed a VCR, latest estimates reveal that more than half (55 per cent) of individuals and nearly seven out of ten people with children (69 per cent) have acquired a VCR (IBA, 1988).

There is no doubt that, from early on, the desire existed among the public to have direct access to a piece of equipment which adds a new dimension of personal control over viewing and can significantly change the way the television set is used. In 1979, for instance, when asked about their preferences either for a teletext television receiver which "can show you written information on a television screen about all sorts of subjects just by pressing a button" or for a television recorder which "can be used to record and play back television programmes", 56 per cent of a national survey sample in Britain opted for the television recorder, compared with

13 per cent who preferred a teletext receiver, and 13 per cent who did not know. A further 18 per cent wanted neither (IBA, 1979).

Characteristics of VCR owners

The spread of VCRs has not occurred to the same extent throughout all types of household. As Table 2.1 below shows, penetration occurred most rapidly and extensively among people with children, the young and middle-aged, and among moderate viewers. VCRs have been less popular among people of retirement age and are found less commonly among the unskilled and semi-skilled working classes (DEs).

One anomalous result for which there is no clearcut explanation is the fall in the percentage of 45–54 year olds owning a VCR in 1986 compared to 1985. This may be a consequence of sampling fluctuations given that in 1986 the sample size was considerably boosted for this survey because of other special requirements at the time.

Table 2.1. Characteristics of VCR owners

	1980 %	1981 %	1982 %	1984 %	1985 %	1986 %
Households:						
with children	4	10	26	47	51	58
without children	3	7	13	25	29	33
Social class:						
AB	5	15	24	35	40	51
C1	4	8	18	41	41	52
C2	4	9	20	43	45	53
DE	2	4	11	25	28	30
Age:						
16-24	4	11	26	51	49	55
25-34	5	12	23	47	48	58
35-44	2	10	26	44	47	60
45-54	6	11	15	40	56	46
55-64	1	2	10	24	19	38
65+	2	2	4	5	7	11
Amount of TV viewing:						
3+ hours	3	8	17	33	37	40
1-2 hours	5	9	19	40	41	51
less than 1 hour	0	13	19	26	20	44

Source: IBA, Attitudes to Broadcasting Surveys, 1980-1986

So rapid has been the growth of home video, research on its impact and use has been left standing. In the UK, the video phenomenon has had important implications for the measurement of television audiences, since the electronic metering devices used by broadcasters to monitor viewing behaviour could not originally detect video usage. Technological enhancements were needed and had to be speedily developed and implemented in order to correct substantial measurement inaccuracies produced by the outmoded monitoring equipment. We will return to that story later in the chapter.

Despite the additional complexities and problems for television audience measurement introduced by VCRs, certain basic statistics have emerged, largely derived from the self-reports of VCR owners. A VCR can be used either to view bought or hired, pre-recorded films or television programmes as well as to make one's own recordings of programmes broadcast on regular television channels. A VCR can also be used to play back videotape recordings made on home video cameras, although only 2 per cent of VCR households in 1986 had such a camera (IBA, 1987).

"Time-shifting" is the most common mode of VCR usage. In Britain, more than 80 per cent of individuals with a VCR say they use it regularly to record programmes off-air for later viewing at a more convenient time. Around two-thirds claim to have hired a pre-recorded film at some time. The latest estimates presented in Table 2.2 indicate that some 73 per cent say they view self-recorded programmes more than once a week compared with 15 per cent who say the same about hired videos.

Table 2.2. Frequency of video use

	To watch programmes recorded earlier off TV			To watch bought/hired pre-recorded films		
	1984 %	1985 %	1986 %	1984 %	1985 %	1986 %
More than once a week	76	80	73	21	18	15
About once a week	9	11	12	14	10	14
Less than once a week	6	5	7	38	38	35
Hardly ever/never	9	4	9	27	34	36

Source: IBA, Attitudes to Broadcasting, 1984-1986

Types of programmes recorded

Video users have been asked what sorts of programmes they usually record for later viewing. The experience in Britain is that the programmes most popularly recorded off-air tend to be films and soap operas (see Figure 2.1). This is true regardless of age, sex, class or the presence of children in the home, although there are some differences in degree between demographic sub-groups. Table 2.3 provides some details.

FIGURE 2.1 Types of programmes recorded off-air
Households with a VCR

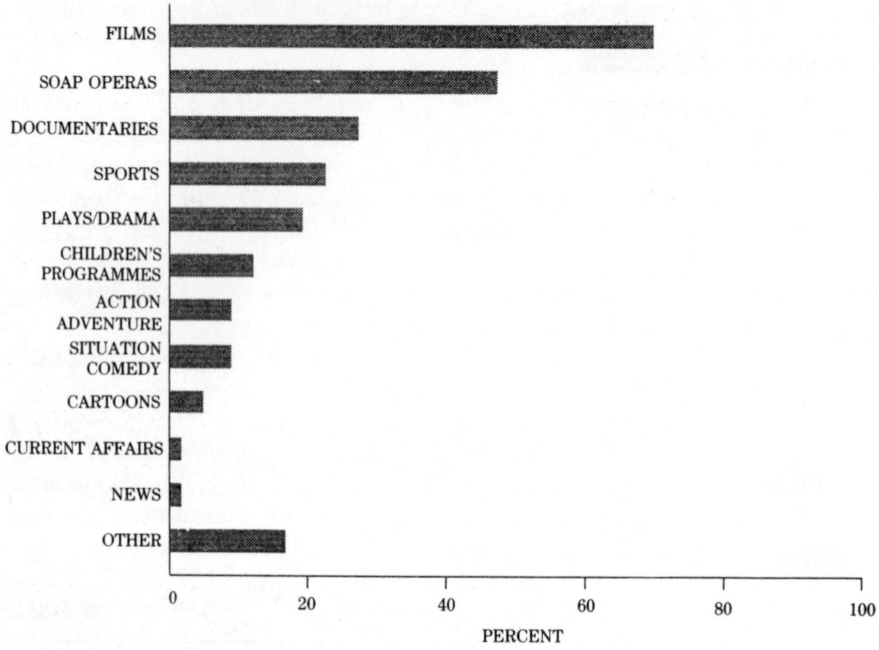

SOURCE: IBA ATTITUDES TO BROADCASTING, 1987

Recording claims for films, for instance, are more common among younger than among older adults. Soap operas are more popular with the young and with women. Older people say they are more likely to record documentaries and men are more likely to record sports. There is also an unsurprising likelihood that children's programmes will be recorded by adults with children (see Figure 2.2).

Some of these findings seem to travel quite well. Levy (1980a), for example, reported from one US sample, that "time-shifting" was the most popular use of home video. The average VCR household in the U.S. made just over four recordings off-air per week, played back between three and four tapes of previously broadcast material, and watched less than one pre-recorded cassette which had been bought, hired or borrowed from outside sources. Movies were recorded and played back most often, followed by situation comedies and soap operas.

FIGURE 2.2 Types of programmes recorded off-air (adults with children)

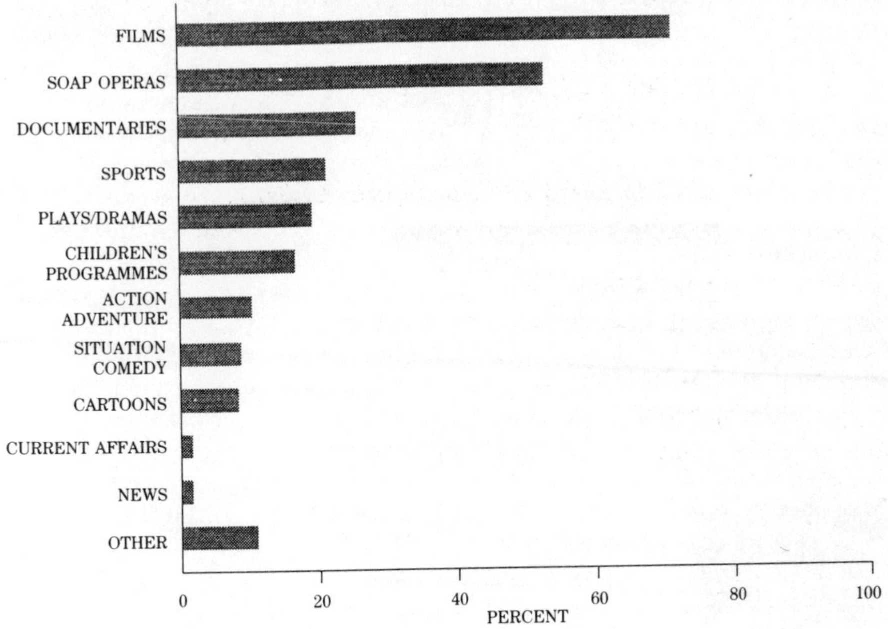

SOURCE: IBA ATTITUDES TO BROADCASTING 1987

Table 2.3. Types of programme recorded

	All with VCR %	AGE 16-34 %	AGE 35-55 %	55+ %	CLASS ABC1 %	CLASS C2DE %	SEX Men %	SEX Women %	Adults with Children
Films	68	71	68	56	64	71	67	68	70
'Soap Operas'	46	56	40	34	44	48	34	56	51
Documentaries	27	18	35	32	29	25	29	25	25
Sports	22	18	25	24	20	24	29	16	20
Plays/Drama	18	16	19	22	23	14	15	20	18
Adventure/Police	9	10	7	10	9	9	11	8	10
Children's Programmes	11	16	9	3	12	10	8	14	17
Comedy	8	8	9	6	10	7	10	6	8
Cartoons	5	8	4	1	5	6	5	6	8
Current Affairs	2	1	4	3	3	2	4	1	2
News	2	1	3	1	1	2	2	1	2
Other types/not classifiable	16	10	8	13	10	9	10	10	10
'It depends'	2	3	4	8	4	4	6	3	3

Source: IBA, Attitudes to Broadcasting, 1987. Multiple responses allowed.

Impact of VCR on conventional TV viewing

Descriptive statistics concerning the penetration and use of video recorders paint a remarkable picture of a rapidly changing media environment. However, what is perhaps an even more interesting issue and one of considerable importance to broadcasters, concerns the impact the VCR has had and is having on conventional television viewing.

In Britain this became an especially sensitive issue when the Broadcasters Audience Research Board (BARB) reported a large fall-off in viewing in the autumn of 1982. Was it caused by VCR usage? At the time, BARB did not have the technical facility to measure VCR impact on television viewing. Quickly, however, it became known that people were widely using their VCR as a tuner during live TV viewing. Individuals with a remote control for their VCR who did not have one for their TV set could and often did choose to view using the VCR as the receiver, giving them a remote channel switching capability while watching material off-air. Since the electronic viewing meters ceased to function when the VCR was used in this way, these "live" viewers were lost to the system and were recorded as non-viewers.

A BARB special analysis, issued in 1982, attempted to explain the extent to which viewing losses could be attributed to VCR use (BARB, 1982). This assessment concluded that up to half of the "loss" in live viewing was probably due to video usage. BARB estimated that 2 per cent of the decline in hours of viewing per home, could be accounted for in terms of live viewing via the VCR tuner, 1 per cent in terms of time-shift viewing of self-recorded programmes and half a per cent in terms of watching pre-recorded tapes.

Accounting for viewing losses after the fact in this way was one thing, but it was important to have some form of continuous monitoring of VCR usage and the extent to which it impinged on live television viewing. A number of developments ensued during the next year or two. First, VCR ownership became a control for respondent selection so that at least the representative nature of the basic sample could be assured. Until the beginning of 1983, "other uses of the TV set" (i.e. VCR, home computers, video games) were measured by the meter but it was not possible to distinguish VCR use, so arrangements were made to develop means of capturing total VCR use from the meter. This, however, gave only a measure of total VCR use and did not distinguish between the three main elements, i.e. live viewing through the VCR, time-shift viewing and viewing of pre-recorded material.

The major problem was time-shift viewing – how to identify the programme being replayed. A method for encoding off-air broadcasts electronically so that they could be identified by the meters was suggested, but found to be too complex and expensive. As an alternative, a special diary was issued to all BARB panel homes with a VCR in March 1983. Panelists were required to record the time and incidence of all viewing via their VCR, and to distinguish between live viewing, time-shift viewing and viewing of pre-recorded tapes. In the case of time-shift, the programme and date/time/channel of the original transmission had to be recorded, as well as the time it was viewed.

The experiment, however, was not an unqualified success. First the rate of acceptance of diaries by VCR homes and rate of return were lower than had been hoped for, with the result that the diary data were based on approximately 75 per cent of BARB VCR homes. A second problem was that a significant proportion of time registered on the meter as VCR use did not have a corresponding diary entry. This "unallocated" time ranged from 0.4 hours up to a maximum of 2.5 hours per home per week, averaging about 1.5 hours per week – some 25 per cent of metered VCR usage.

Other results indicated that the level of "live" viewing using the VCR as a tuner/receiver was around one hour a week per VCR home; somewhat lower during summer months, and lower overall than had been expected. Around three to four hours a week were occupied by viewing of self-recorded, time-shift programmes. And around one and a half to two hours a week were devoted to watching pre-recorded tapes.

The problem of the unallocated time was probably due to unrecorded live viewing using the VCR as a tuner. The reason for this was most likely that viewers did not always remember to make a note of such viewing since they routinely used the VCR as the signal receiver.

A further study reported by BARB (1984) examined the frequency and delay of playing back self-recorded programmes. A sub-sample of the national viewing panel who were VCR owners kept a VCR diary for four weeks. Results indicated that 87 per cent of all self-recorded programmes were played back at least once, 13 per cent were played back at least twice and 5 per cent at least three times. A further 13 per cent were not played back. Most self-recordings replayed (93 per cent) were played back within seven days.

These surveys, however, have only just begun to scratch the surface of knowledge about video usage. VCRs may lead viewers to believe they have greater personal control over their use of the TV set than ever before. Viewers can now re-schedule programmes, instead of being restricted to original broadcast schedules; they can even build their own schedules by drawing upon home tape libraries to enhance their choice of viewing fare (see Levy, 1980a).

Although we already know a few things about how home video is used, little research has yet been done to demonstrate how, if at all, the presence of a VCR changes the structure of home viewing. VCRs in Britain are especially common in family households, where they can have

11

special functions as a source of entertainment and information for the whole family. In this monograph, we report a detailed study of home video usage among VCR households in England with the spotlight focused on aspects of the social context of video viewing in homes with and without children. Let us introduce that study here.

A detailed study of home video use

The investigation monitored a sample of video households over a period of time to learn how the VCR is used in the context of normal, everyday television viewing. The aim was to obtain a detailed log of video recording and viewing behaviour and to probe users' attitudes towards their videos. We wanted to find out how often people used their VCRs and what their intentions usually were with regard to the programmes they record. Did most VCR households keep a limited supply of tapes which they used over and over again, such that each recording had a short life span? Or did some VCR users build their own library of movies and favourite television programmes? What did users perceive to be the main advantages of having a VCR? And in what ways were users dissatisfied with it?

Contacts were made with 500 VCR households in four Independent Television Regions in England – London, Midlands, North-West England, and Yorkshire. The sample was an interlocking quota sample based on sex, six age and four social-class groups. Usable diaries and question-naires were received from 446 households – for a response rate of 89 per cent.

Respondents filled out two questionnaires and two, one-week TV viewing diaries over two consecutive weeks. The contact questionnaire was designed to establish (1) VCR ownership or rental; (2) demographic information concerning sex, age, social class, working status, marital status, presence and age of children in household, and age at which full-time education ended; (3) media availability and usage, including number of TV sets, type of TV set, possession of home computer, connection to cable TV, frequency of newspaper and magazine reading, radio listening, and cinema attendance. On the second questionnaire, respondents assessed TV, radio, video, cinema, newspapers, records/tapes as enter-taining, informative, and providing variety of content, and were asked about length of VCR ownership/rental, video camera ownership, number of blank cassettes in home, recency and frequency of purchasing or hiring cassettes, types of cassettes bought or hired, usual intended use if self-recorded cassettes, size of tape library and attitudes towards home video.

Each seven-day diary ran from Monday to Sunday. For each day, a complete programme listing was presented for each of the four broadcast TV channels (BBC1, BBC2, ITV and Channel Four) together with a video (playback) section in which respondents were requested to write in the names of the video-recorded programmes they watched that day. Respondents were required to supply three categories of information about each programme: programme appreciation, if the programme was viewed; whether they recorded the programme; and if they viewed alone or with someone else. Two programme evaluations were made. Respondents were asked to give each programme a score out of ten for enjoyment and for strength of impression. (An analysis of appreciation data will be presented in a subsequent report.) Next, respondents indicated for any programme, whether viewed at the time or not, if they recorded it. They were also asked about their intended use of the recording, for which four response options were supplied: (1) play back this week, then erase; (2) play back this week, then save for collection; (3) will not play back this week, but will save for collection; and (4) may erase or save, not certain right now. Finally, for social context of viewing, respondents indicated if they viewed alone, with other adult members of the household, with adult visitors, or with child visitors.

On the video viewing (playback) page each day, respondents wrote in the name of any taped programme watched, the start and finish times of viewing for each entered title, whether the tape was self-recorded during the last seven days or longer ago, or whether it was a purchased or hired pre-recorded cassette, and finally the social context of viewing as above.

Contacts with the sampled households were made three times. On initial recruitment, respondents were given a five-minute interview with the first questionnaire and then the first week's viewing diary was placed with them. The diary was explained to respondents so that they fully understood how to complete it. At the end of the first week, interviewers called again to place the second week's diary and to check that respondents were filling out the information requested from them each day. Within two days of the end of the second week, interviewers paid a final visit to each household to conduct a 15-minute interview with the second questionnaire and to collect both TV-video diaries.

Demographic characteristics

The modal VCR household was composed of two adults, with two-thirds (66.4 per cent) of all VCR households containing at least one child under the age of 16. Almost one-third (32.1 per cent) of VCR households had at least one child aged 4–9 years, and one-fifth (22.2 per cent) had at least one young teenager (ages 13–15). Some 84.5 per cent of VCR owners interviewed were currently married, while one in seven (13.5 per cent) were single. Some 51.8 per cent of VCR users sampled had left school at age 16. Around four out of ten (40.8 per cent) VCR owners was a member of the skilled working class (C2), while 42.8 per cent were classified as from the professional, middle classes (AB = 29.4 per cent, C1 = 12.8 per cent), and 16.4 per cent were semi-skilled or unskilled working-class (D or E).

Media use

Nearly three-quarters (71.5 per cent) of VCR households sampled had two or more TV sets, and almost three in ten (29.4 per cent) had a home computer. Only 1.6 per cent of VCR households in this sample had cable TV. More than one-third (35.9 per cent) rented their VCR. The median length of time that video had been in the household was two to three years, with about one in five (20.1 per cent) having had a video for a year or less and one in seven (14.3 per cent) for more than four years. Only one in twenty-five (4.2 per cent) had a video camera.

Most respondents (66.9 per cent) read a newspaper at least five or six times in the "past week", with a slightly higher proportion (70.5 per cent) listening to the radio five or six times during that week for at least ten minutes. The modal (43.2 per cent) VCR user interviewed did not regularly read any magazines during the course of a month, although one-third (32.1 per cent) read one or two. A substantial proportion (80.4 per cent) of respondents had not gone out to the cinema even once in the three months before the interview, while most of the remainder had seen only one or two movies outside their home.

Attitudes towards home video

The growth of home video has been phenomenal but what is the attraction of having a VCR? Once a VCR has been acquired, what do users think about it? How does it compare with other media? And what special advantages accompany having a VCR?

Comparisons of media attributes

Respondents were asked to compare television, radio, video, cinema, newspapers, and records/audio tapes on qualities of "entertaining", "informative", and "variety of content". Rank orders, based on a five-point scale of "most" = 1 to "least" = 6 are shown in Table 2.4.

Video entertainment is clearly well-liked, though many users would like to have more choice of offerings. When asked to compare video with television, radio, newspapers, cinema and records/audio tapes on qualities of "entertaining", video was rated second after television. Interestingly, cinema was ranked the least entertaining. Not surprisingly,

Table 2.4. Comparative ratings of selected media

Entertaining	Informative	Content variety
Television (1.59)	Television (1.69)	Television (1.54)
Video (2.99)	Newspapers (2.05)	Radio (2.89)
Radio (3.24)	Radio (2.54)	Newspapers (3.29)
Records (3.91)	Video (4.44)	Video (3.63)
Newspapers (4.01)	Cinema (5.09)	Records (4.48)
Cinema (5.24)	Records (5.22)	Cinema (5.17)

(Note: Numbers in parentheses are sample means)

video was not rated as a good information source, but perhaps more significant, it finished behind television, radio and newspapers in terms of variety.

Perceived advantages and disadvantages of home video

In addition to measuring video behaviour we wanted to find out about viewers' experience with their videos. Does video provide particular kinds of gratification? And, in contrast, what are the main problems people have with their videos?

Nine items were included in the survey to measure the "uses and gratifications" of home video. It seems that people see a number of clear advantages to having a VCR. The most important thing for most of our VCR householders (95 per cent) was the greater control a VCR gave them over when to watch television programmes and films. For many also, watching a video saved the trouble and expense of going out to the cinema (75 per cent) and was seen as an enjoyable way for the family to spend more time together (74 per cent). These reasons were found to be especially common in homes with children up to the age of 12 years.

The most serious problem people had with their home videos was lacking the time to view all the programmes they had taped themselves (61 per cent). A less serious complaint was finding it difficult to rent pre-recorded tapes they wanted (33 per cent).

In order further to assess the perceived advantages and disadvantages of home video, an analysis was done to examine how video gratifications cluster together and vary across different types of video user and video household.

Responses to the nine gratifications items were factor analysed, and the result was a three-factor solution. The three factors were named: (1) Choice-Family; (2) Social Interaction; and (3) Dissatisfactions. The following table groups the measures by factor on which each load most highly (see Table 2.5).

Table 2.5. Video gratifications

	Strongly Agree %	Agree %	Neither %	Dis- agree %	Strongly Disagree %
Factor 1: Choice-Family					
Greater choice over time of viewing	50	45	3	2	0
Greater choice of content	22	50	9	13	6
Avoid going out to cinema	35	40	7	12	6
Enjoyable family activity	21	53	10	13	3
Need to record serials	36	43	9	9	3
Factor 2: Social Interaction					
Enjoyable with friends	17	30	13	24	16
Bought video to collect tapes	3	5	17	37	38
Factor 3: Dissatisfactions					
Lack time to view tapes made	19	42	5	23	11
Hard to rent tapes want to see	11	22	18	31	18

(A tenth item in this battery but excluded from the factor analysis measured an aspect of audience activity, that is the degree to which the use of a VCR to tape off-air represents a purposive behaviour. About one-fifth (22.2 per cent) of respondents agreed strongly that they "carefully plan" what they are going to tape, while an additional 44.1 per cent agreed. Some 9.9 per cent neither agreed nor disagreed, while 17.3 per cent disagreed that off-air recording was carefully planned and 6.2 per cent strongly disagreed.)

Based on the three factors extracted above, factor scales were created and predictors of support for these summative scales then examined.

Choice-Family
Support for this dimension was significantly and positively associated (based on one-dimensional contingency table analysis) with the presence of children aged 4–9 or 10–12 years in the household. Support for the Choice-Family dimension declined with respondent age, and was not significantly associated with respondent sex, class, or length of VCR ownership.

Social Interaction
At the bivariate level, there were few measures significantly associated

with this dimension. Respondent sex, age, class and length of VCR ownership were not statistically related. However, support for this scale did significantly increase with the presence of one or more children, aged 4–9, and was higher for those respondents who had never bought a pre-recorded video.

Dissatisfactions

Support for this dissatisfaction dimension was roughly uniform across the entire sample. No significant differences were found by demographic variables. However, people who had "never" rented a video were significantly more likely to endorse this factor.

None of the bivariate relationships reported above for the three factor-scales was affected by separate second-order controls for either social class or the presence of children in the household.

Summary

The 1980s witnessed the rapid spread of VCRs in the United Kingdom. From negligible penetration in 1979, ownership grew until by the middle of the decade more than half of adults, and nearly seven out of ten of those with children living at home, had acquired a VCR (IBA, 1988).

VCRs are used mainly for time-shifting. In other words, programmes are recorded off the main television channels to be played back relatively soon at a more convenient time. Practically all VCR users have made their own recordings at one time or another. A majority also say they have at some time hired or bought (usually the former) a pre-recorded videotape (IBA, 1987).

National surveys have revealed that the most popularly recorded programmes are films and soap operas. In households with children, children's programmes also feature fairly prominently (IBA, 1987).

The acquisition and use of VCRs happened so quickly that it outstripped technological developments needed to effectively measure television audiences on a routine basis. Audience sizes for television programmes in the UK are projected from the viewing habits of a representative national panel of households who have electronic meters attached to their television sets recording when the set is switched on and to which channel it is tuned. Many video households used their VCRs as tuners for their television set, with the television signal received through the VCR rather than by the set aerial. Electronic meters originally did not function when the VCR was used in this way. These "live" viewers therefore were lost to the system, and viewing levels appeared to fail. Now new meters have been developed to cope with this problem.

Although certain basic data about VCR usage have been available for the UK, until now a detailed analysis of continuous VCR usage has been lacking. This chapter introduces a survey which focused on video behaviour in a sample of VCR households in four ITV regions. Diaries were placed with householders in which they kept a record of off-air television viewing, any video recordings made and video playbacks watched. In the diaries, VCR owners were also asked to indicate their intended use of personal recordings, the type of videotape played back (self-recorded or pre-recorded) and with whom they watched. In addition, two questionnaire interviews were carried out to obtain background information about the respondents themselves, about their attitudes toward home video and about the nature of use of their household's VCR.

Video homes are mostly family households with two adults and at least one child aged under 16 years. VCR households are well-equipped in other ways too: nearly three out of four in our survey had more than one television set compared with a national average of just over 50 per cent, and about one in three had a home computer.

Video entertainment was clearly well-liked, though many users said they would like to have more choice on offer. When asked to compare video with television, radio, newspapers, cinema and records/audio tapes on qualities of "entertaining", "informative" and "variety of content", video was rated as the second most entertaining medium after television. Not surprisingly, video was not rated as a good information source, but perhaps more significantly, it finished behind television, radio and newspapers in terms of variety.

We asked users about their experience with video. Does video provide particular kinds of gratification? Is it perceived to offer particular benefits or to serve special purposes? And in contrast, what are the main problems or sources of disatisfaction people have with their videos?

It seems that people see a number of clear advantages to having a VCR. The most important, our sample reports, is the greater control a VCR gives them over when to watch television programmes and films. For many also, watching a video was seen as an enjoyable way for the family to spend some time together and as a way to save the trouble and expense of going out to the cinema. These reasons were found to be especially common in homes with children up to the age of 12 years.

The most serious problem people had with their home videos was their own lack of time to view all the programmes they themselves had taped. A less serious complaint was finding it difficult to rent pre-recorded tapes they wanted to watch.

Summing up then, home video seems to be a welcome new technology which gives viewers an unprecedented degree of personal control over how they watch television. Video is enjoyed especially in family homes where regular viewing of self-recorded programmes off television is a popular pastime and the VCR is seen as a cheap and convenient way to entertain younger members of the household.

CHAPTER THREE

VIEWING, RECORDING AND PLAYBACK PROFILES IN VIDEO HOUSEHOLDS

In this chapter we examine some of the basic characteristics of home video behaviour, drawing upon both the self-reported video behaviours and diary records of respondents. We consider self-estimates of recency and frequency of off-air taping, tape rental and tape purchase, intended use of self-recorded material, and number and type of self-recordings and video playbacks. We compare the distribution across programme types of video viewing and live television viewing. Are those programme types that are the most viewed at the time of transmission also those most watched as video playbacks? Finally, we look at whether and how video users deal with advertising breaks in programmes they have recorded. If the user is present when a recording is being made, is any attempt made electronically to "cut" out the commercials? Or, if commercials are recorded along with the programme, as would happen if the recording is controlled by an automatic timing mechanism with which most VCRs are equipped, are advertising breaks skipped at playback by pressing the fast-forward button?

Self-reported video behaviours

Off-air taping
Some 98.9 per cent of respondents said they had "ever" made video recordings off-air. More than half (54.5 per cent) said they "generally" recorded over the tape once they had watched the programmes, while 40.8 per cent said they generally kept recordings for "a while" and 4.7 per cent said they generally kept their recordings for a library.

Keeping tapes in a home video library was significantly related to social class. Almost two-thirds (65.4 per cent) of AB respondents said they "ever" kept tapes they had made off-air for a home library, while only about one-third (34–38 per cent) of all other respondents said they were building even small video library collections. Having a video library was not significantly associated with respondent sex or age, or with the presence of children in the household.

Video rental

Nearly nine out of ten (89.6 per cent) VCR households had "ever" rented a pre-recorded tape. More than one-third (37.4 per cent) had rented a tape within the "last 7 days" and another 30.3 per cent had rented a tape within the "last month". More than one-quarter (29.5 per cent) of households *generally* rented a tape "once a week or more often", with 18.5 per cent renting two or three times a month and 18.7 per cent once a month. Almost all rentals (95.6 per cent) were of movies.

Frequency of rentals declined with respondent age. For example, while 69.2 per cent of respondents 16–24 years of age and 47.7 per cent of respondents aged 25–34 rented at least one tape within the "last" month, only 22.2 per cent of respondents aged 55–64 showed a similar rental pattern. Further, social class ABC1 respondents were about 10 per cent less likely to have ever rented a tape than respondents in classes C2, D or E. Video rental was not significantly linked to respondent sex or the presence of children in the household.

Video purchases

About one-quarter (23.6 per cent) of VCR households had "ever" purchased a pre-recorded video cassette. One in four (26.9 per cent) had made such a purchase within the "last" month, while the most common interval of tape purchasing (43.6 per cent) was "less than once a year". Some 60.2 per cent of tapes bought were of movies, while most of the remainder (23.3 per cent of the total) were of "pop videos".

The heaviest buyers of videos were members of social class C2. Some 31.8 per cent had "ever" bought a pre-recorded video, compared to only 14.5 per cent of AB respondents and 19.8 per cent of C1-type users. Tape purchases were not significantly associated with respondent sex, age or the presence of children in the household.

There were variations in the way respondents claimed to use their videos which coincided with the length of time they had had a VCR. While practically all respondents recorded programmes off television regardless of how long they had had a VCR, the likelihood of renting or buying pre-recorded cassettes and of keeping self-recorded tapes for a personal library all increased with length of ownership.

Attitudes to video and claimed use

As we reported in the last chapter, respondents were questioned about their attitudes to home video. We were interested to find out about perceived benefits and dissatisfactions with video, and the main functions or purposes users believed it to serve. A range of benefits and some problems were extensively endorsed. In this section we examine how these attitudes were related to self-reported video behaviours.

Only one attitude that we measured discriminated to any marked degree between whether or not pre-recorded videotapes were purchased at all. More than half (53 per cent) of those respondents who agreed that watching a video is an enjoyable way to spend time with friends said that they had at some time purchased pre-recorded videotapes. Video-related attitudes made little difference to recency of last purchase or frequency with which purchases of pre-recorded tapes are normally made.

However, attitudes proved to be better indicators of pre-recorded tape rentals. Renting of pre-recorded tapes was much more commonplace among our sample of video householders than was the purchase of such tapes. However, the perception that having a VCR served particular functions was related to whether respondents rented tapes at all, how often and when they last did so.

Table 3.1 shows that three attitude items emerged as predictors of whether respondents had ever rented pre-recorded tapes. In two cases, the level of differentation was quite substantial. Respondents who had rented pre-recorded tapes before were more likely than those who had not to agree; (1) that having a VCR saves the trouble and expense of going out to the cinema; (2) that compared to television video adds to the viewing choice; (3) and that it is often difficult to find those pre-recorded tapes they most want to see.

Attitudes were also related in some cases to the recency with which respondents last rented a pre-recorded tape. For the purpose of this comparison, we divided respondents into three categories: those who last rented a tape less than seven days ago, those who had rented longer than a week ago but within the last month, and those who had not rented a tape for more than one month.

There was a greater tendency for recent renters, compared with non-recent renters, to agree; (1) that watching video is an enjoyable way to spend time with family and friends; (2) that compared to television, video offers greater choice; (3) that video can be a cheap convenient substitute for going out to the cinema; (4) and not surprisingly given their more active rental behaviours that it is often difficult to get hold of the tapes they really want to see. Recent renters were less likely than non-recent renters, however, to complain that they often had difficulty finding the time to watch all the recorded programmes they have taped (see Table 3.2).

21

Table 3.1. Attitudes to video and renting pre-recorded tapes

Percent Agreeing with Statement	Whether Rent Pre-Recorded Tapes	
	Yes %	No %
Having a VCR saves one the trouble and expense of going out to the cinema	79	58
Compared to television, video gives me a greater choice of things to watch	73	65
It is often difficult to rent the pre-recorded tapes that I really want to see	38	19

Table 3.2. Attitudes to video and recency of last pre-recorded tape rental

Percent Agreeing with Statement	Less than 7 days ago %	Less than 1 month ago %	More than 1 month ago %
Watching a video is often an enjoyable way for my family to spend some time together	80	71	70
Watching a video is often an enjoyable way for me and my friends to spend some time together	46	46	37
Compared to television, video gives me a greater choice of things to watch	75	71	69
Having a VCR saves me the trouble and expense of going out to the cinema	82	81	70
It is often difficult for me to find the time to watch all the programmes I have taped	53	64	64
It is often difficult to rent the pre-recorded tapes that I really want to see	40	39	36

These same attitudes were related in a similar fashion to reported frequencies of renting pre-recorded tapes. Once again, respondents were divided into three categories: those who claimed usually to rent tapes at least once a week, those who claimed to do at least once a month and those who rented less often than once a month.

Frequent renters were more likely than relatively infrequent renters to agree that watching a video provides an enjoyable occasion to spend with family or friends, and that it saves the trouble and expense of going out to the cinema. Frequent renters were somethat less likely than infrequent renters to say they often had difficulty finding the time to watch videos (see Table 3.3).

Table 3.3: Attitudes to video and frequency of pre-recorded tape rentals

	Frequency of Pre-Recorded Tape Rental		
Percent Agreeing with Statement	**At least once a week** %	**At least once a month** %	**Less often than once a month** %
Watching a video is often an enjoyable way for my family to spend some time together	83	74	65
Watching a video is often an enjoyable way for me and my friends to spend some time together	50	47	35
Having a VCR saves me the trouble and expense of going out to the cinema	84	77	72
It is often difficult for me to find the time to watch all the programmes I have taped	55	59	62

Number and intended use of self-recordings

The mean number of self-recordings per VCR household across the two survey weeks was 3.76. Fewer recordings were made during the second week (Average = 3.51) than the first (Average = 4.00). This slight decline most likely represents some small degree of panel fatigue. But since we generally report 2-week averages, this decline has no substantive significance. Slightly fewer self-recordings were made in homes with children during the first week, while there was essentially no difference during the second week.

The predominant intention with regard to most self-recordings was to play back the programme within the week and then to re-use the video tape. This accounted for three-quarters of all self-recordings. Only about one in ten recordings were intended to be saved (see Table 3.4).

Number of self- and pre-recorded video playbacks

The mean number of video playbacks over the two weeks was 2.59 per week. As with the number of self-recordings that were made, the number

23

Table 3.4: Number and intended use of self-recordings

	Week One			Week Two		
	All Homes	Homes without Children	Homes with Children	All Homes	Homes without Children	Homes with Children
Total number of programmes recorded	4.00	4.33	3.99	3.51	3.49	3.52
Intended use of recording:	%	%	%	%	%	%
1. Play back this week, then erase	75	74	75	76	73	77
2. Play back this week, then save	7	5	8	3	2	5
3. Will not play this week, but save	4	4	3	3	5	2
4. Not certain	14	17	14	18	20	16

FIGURE 3.1 Breakdown of video playbacks

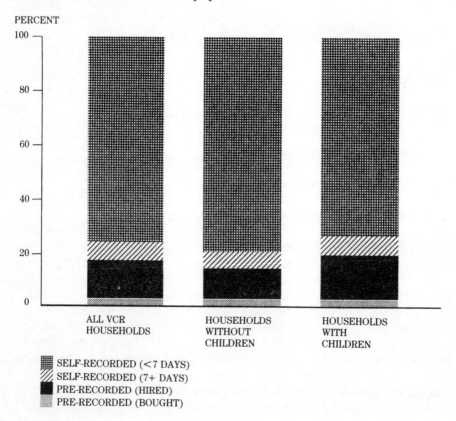

PERCENT

ALL VCR HOUSEHOLDS

HOUSEHOLDS WITHOUT CHILDREN

HOUSEHOLDS WITH CHILDREN

SELF-RECORDED (<7 DAYS)
SELF-RECORDED (7+ DAYS)
PRE-RECORDED (HIRED)
PRE-RECORDED (BOUGHT)

24

of playbacks decreased from week one to week two (see Table 3.5). More than four out of five playbacks were of self-recorded material, most of which had been made within the last seven days. Of pre-recorded tapes played back, most had been hired. Few purchased videos were played back. A graphic representation of the breakdown of video playbacks is shown in Figure 3.1.

The presence of children in the household made some small differences to the type of material played back. A greater proportion of video playbacks in homes with children were self-recordings and a smaller proportion were of hired pre-recorded tapes.

Table 3.5: Number of self-recorded and pre-recorded video playbacks

	Week One			*Week Two*		
	All Homes	Homes without Children	Homes with Children	All Homes	Homes without Children	Homes with Children
Total number of video playbacks	2.88	2.75	2.91	2.29	1.98	2.47
	%	%	%	%	%	%
Self-recorded (total)	84	89	84	82	84	82
Pre-recorded (total)	16	11	16	18	16	18
Type of Self Recording						
Self-recorded (<7 days)	75	81	76	76	81	74
Self-recorded (7+ days)	9	9	8	6	3	8
Type of Pre-Recording						
Pre-recorded (bought)	1	2	1	1	1	1
Pre-recorded (hired)	15	8	15	17	15	17

Types of programmes viewed, recorded and played back

Table 3.6 shows the breakdown of TV viewing, self-recorded and video playback material by programme types. This typology was based on standard industry programme categories used by BARB. Across the two survey weeks, the three programme types *viewed* most often off-air were news (19 per cent of total programmes viewed), quiz and game shows (12 per cent) and UK drama serials (about 12 per cent). The three programme types most often self-recorded were US drama series (15 per cent of total self recordings), children's programmes (12 per cent) and UK drama serials and films/TV movies (both 11 per cent). Programme types most often played back on video, however, were different again. The three most popular were UK drama series (16 per cent of total video playbacks), films/TV movies (14 per cent) and UK drama serials (12 per cent).

Table 3.6: Types of programmes viewed off-air recorded and played back

Programme type	Seen on: TV		Self-recorded Off-air		Video Playback	
	Week 1 %	Week 2 %	Week 1 %	Week 2 %	Week 1 %	Week 2 %
UK-drama series	6	7	8	7	7	24
UK-drama serials	12	11	13	9	13	11
US-drama series	5	10	8	21	9	7
US-drama serials	4	4	8	5	9	10
Films/TV movies	4	4	11	10	13	15
Music and variety	5	5	9	6	5	5
Situation comedy	9	7	10	7	11	7
Quiz and game shows	12	12	4	6	3	4
Chat shows	3	3	1	2	5	3
News	18	19	3	4	0	0
Sport	6	4	3	3	4	4
Documentaries	9	7	13	7	8	7
Serious music/arts	1	1	0	0	1	0
Children's TV	6	6	9	13	12	3

Table 3.7 shows the programme type breakdown of self-recordings and video playbacks for households with and without children. In homes without children, the most popularly self-recorded programme types were US drama series, film/TV movies and documentaries. In homes with

FIGURE 3.2 Types of programmes viewed off-air

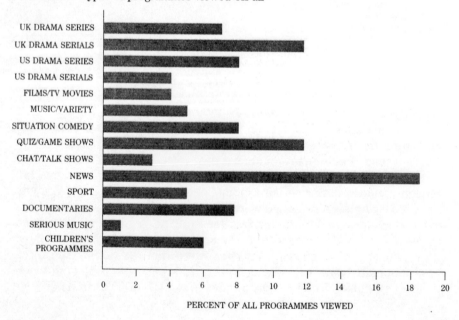

PERCENT OF ALL PROGRAMMES VIEWED

26

FIGURE 3.3 Types of programmes recorded off-air

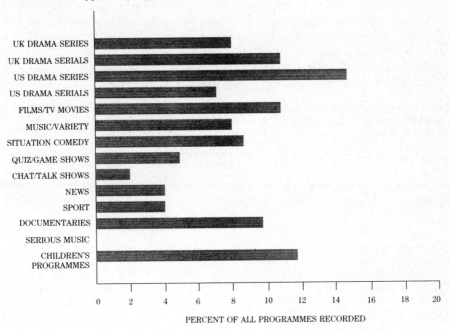

PERCENT OF ALL PROGRAMMES RECORDED

FIGURE 3.4 Types of programmes played back

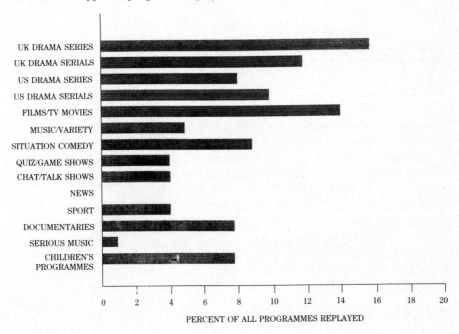

PERCENT OF ALL PROGRAMMES REPLAYED

children, although US drama series were popular once again, UK drama serials and children's programmes were also often recorded. The most popular playback material was UK drama series, films/TV movies and UK drama serials. In addition, in homes with children, children's programmes featured prominently among video playbacks. (The extent to which different types of programmes were recorded and viewed off-air and as playbacks is also shown in Figures 3.2, 3.3 and 3.4.)

Table 3.7: Types of programmes recorded and played-back in households with and without children

Programme type	Self-Recorded		Video Playbacks	
	Homes without Children %	Homes with Children %	Homes without Children %	Homes with Children %
UK-drama series	9	7	16	17
UK-drama serials	10	11	12	12
US-drama series	14	15	7	9
US-drama serials	7	6	11	9
Films/TV movies	13	9	17	13
Music and variety	8	7	7	4
Situation comedy	7	9	9	9
Quiz and game shows	6	5	4	3
Chat Shows	2	1	3	3
News	3	4	1	0
Sport	2	5	2	5
Documentaries	11	9	7	7
Serious Music/arts	0	0	1	1
Children's TV	8	12	3	8

Sex differences*

Comparisons between men and women on self-reported video behaviours and diary measures of viewing and video recording behaviours included some interesting differences. There was mixed support, however, for the observations of other researchers that men tried to dominate the use of home video equipment (Gray, 1986; Morley, 1986).

There were no differences between the sexes of any significance in the frequency or extent of self-reported purchase or rental of pre-recorded video cassettes, with two exceptions. As Table 3.8 shows, the extent to which men and women claimed to be the person in the household who generally buys or rents the most pre-recorded cassettes differed. Men were far more likely than women to say that they personally acquired the

*The authors wish to thank Mallory Wober for pointing out these differences.

most pre-recorded videotapes for viewing at home. Women, on the other hand, were much more likely than men to say that most purchases or rentals of pre-recorded tapes were done by their spouses.

Although self-reported video behaviours revealed one pattern of sex differences, diary measures, which reflect a more continuous monitoring of viewing and recording behaviour, indicated a different one. Table 3.9 shows how many programmes were viewed and recorded off-air and played back by men and women respondents over the two weeks for which diaries were kept. These data show that on average women watched, recorded and played back more off-air television broadcasts than men. Thus, on the evidence of continuously self-monitored behaviour, women do not appear to lag behind in their personal use of home video.

Table 3.8: Who in the household generally buys/rents the most pre-recorded cassettes

Base:	Buy		Rent	
Those who buy/rent	Men %	Women %	Men %	Women %
I do	59	37	60	43
Spouse does	13	27	20	35
Son does	11	14	13	12
Daughter does	6	6	3	4
Other/DK	11	17	5	6

Table 3.9: Numbers of programmes seen live, recorded off-air, and played back by men and women

	Men			Women		
Weeks	1	2	Average	1	2	Average
Over all types						
Number seen live	35.1	29.8	32.4	35.8	31.6	33.7
Number self-recorded	1.7	0.9	1.3	2.6	1.7	2.2
Number played back	1.3	0.7	1.0	2.1	1.3	1.7

These results are interesting not only because of the sex differences in video use which they illustrate, but also because of the discrepancy between reported or claimed behaviour (as revealed in their question-naire interviews) and implicitly disclosed behaviour (ascertained through their diary logs). Self-reported or claimed accounts of behaviour indicate that men buy and rent videotapes more often than women do, thus supporting the hypothesis of male dominance posited elsewhere (Gray, 1986; Morley, 1986). The diary records, however, show that women not only watch more, live, than men do, but that they also record more and play back more.

Self-recording and playback of one's own recordings are clearly not the same as buying or renting, and viewing, pre-recorded cassettes. So it is possible that men are more involved than women in bringing in material from outside the home. But this does not simply substantiate the male domination of home video hypothesis. This is because the present survey indicates that over television output in general, women record and playback more than men do.

Source of programmes recorded

In keeping with general patterns of audience ratings among the four channels in the U.K., ITV was the leading source for off-air video recordings. Almost half (47.6 per cent) of all recordings made during the two-week diary period were of programmes broadcast by ITV, with one-third (33.4 per cent) of all recordings coming from BBC1. Of the remainder, roughly the same proportion were of BBC2 or Channel Four programmes.

Table 3.10: Sources of off-air recordings by channel

	BBC1 %	BBC2 %	ITV %	Channel Four %	
Week 1	34.6	10.0	45.8	9.6	100.0
Week 2	32.0	10.1	49.8	8.1	100.0
2-Week Average	33.4	10.1	47.6	8.9	100.0

Moreover, it appears that there is a moderately strong relationship between the number of programmes *viewed* on a given channel and the number of programmes *recorded* from that channel. The correlation, for

Table 3.11: Pearson correlations between channels viewed and source of off-air recordings

Channel Viewed	BBC1	Channel Recorded BBC2	ITV	Channel Four
BBC1	0.321[a]	0.167[a]	0.046	0.163[b]
BBC2	0.183[a]	0.415[a]	0.097[c]	0.173[a]
ITV	0.150[b]	-0.020	0.297[a]	0.089
Channel Four	0.184[a]	0.099[c]	0.127[b]	0.482

[a] $p < 0.001$
[b] $p < 0.01$
[c] $p < 0.05$

example, between the number of broadcasts viewed on Channel 4 and the number of programmes taped from Channel 4 is a striking 0.482. Similarly, although somewhat less robust, the correlation between the number of programmes viewed and the number of programmes recorded from BBC2 is 0.415; from BBC1, 0.321; and from ITV, 0.297.

Consistency of programmes replayed

Echoing the results of an earlier study conducted in the United States (Levy, 1980a), we found that video households in the U.K. tended to replay recordings of programmes only from a relatively limited number of programme types or genres. For example, of those households replaying at least one off-air recording during diary week 1, more than one-third (34.9 per cent) limited their replays to one programme type. Further, during the same period, 28.4 per cent replayed taped programmes from only two different programme types and 15.1 per cent viewed tapes from three different programme categories. A similar 15.5 per cent replayed programmes from four or five different genres, with all but a handful of the remainder choosing from no more than seven different programme types.

The degree to which a given household replayed programmes of a single programme type was further measured by an Index of Replay Consistency. For each household viewing at least one replay, the index was calculated as the ratio of the total number of replays falling into the modal programme type for the household to the total number of household replays. Scores on the index ranged from 0.00, indicating complete diversity in replay choices, to 1.00, suggesting that the household replayed only programmes of a single type.

The mean score on the Index of Replay Consistency for all households viewing at least one playback during diary week 1 was 0.77 and for households watching at least two or more replays, 0.52.

Table 3.12: Index of replay consistency by programme type

Type of programme	Index of Consistency
UK-originated drama series	0.77
UK-originated drama serials	0.75
Non-UK originated drama series	0.83
Non-UK originated drama serials	0.71
Feature films/TV movies	0.77
Variety and Musicals	0.83
Situation Comedies	0.77
Mean of All Programme Types	0.77

Overall, these results give further support to the notion that VCR households have strong patterns of programme preferences and that video owners tend to "specialise" to a large degree in the type of programme they choose to record and replay. Moreover, the type of programme most frequently replayed (i.e. the modal replay category) does not appear to have any substantial impact on index scores. In short, these findings suggest that despite its potential for increasing the range of programmes viewed, video is not being used by most owners to increase the diversity of broadcasts watched.

Time of day and video playback

We have seen already that people believe video gives them greater control over viewing and a wider choice of what to watch. Does this mean, however, that video playback viewing occurs at different times from off-air television viewing? Or are video playbacks mostly watched at normal viewing times?

We computed the extent to which video users in our sample watched their video playbacks at different times of the day. The day was divided into six dayparts which took into account major watersheds in the television schedules across the day. Table 3.13 shows the extent to which video playback viewing occurred in each daypart. The per centages in this table are based on actual numbers of playbacks and not on the amount of time occupied by playback viewing. In their diaries, respondents were required to indicate the times at which they started and finished any period of playback viewing. A playback was allocated to a particular daypart if at least 75 per cent of the time for which it was watched fell within that period.

As the Table 3.13 indicates, most playback viewing occurred when most "normal" television viewing is likely to take place, that is after 9 pm. The next most popular playback time was the early hours of the morning.

Table 3.13: Percentages of video playbacks watched at different times of day

	All Homes %	Homes without Children %	Homes with Children %
1 am – 6 am	17	13	20
6 am – 9 am	0	0	0
9 am – 12.50 pm	4	4	4
12.50 pm – 5.50 pm	13	11	15
5.50 pm – 9 pm	13	15	11
9 pm – 1 am	53	57	50

Playback viewing between the hours of 5.50 pm and 1 am was more extensive among homes without resident children than among homes with children. This pattern was reversed for very late night (post 1 am) playback watching, which was more commonplace among householders with children. The latter result may reflect a tendency for parents to watch material suitable for adults after the children have gone to bed. The social context of video playback viewing at different times of the day is discussed in more detail in the next chapter.

Recording advertisements in programmes

Broadcasters and advertisers have expressed considerable concern about the deletion or avoidance of television advertisements in programmes that have been video-recorded. Two terms have recently come into fashionable usage to describe this behaviour – "zapping" and "zipping". "Zapping" is the elimination of advertisements while making a recording. "Zipping" is scanning through advertisements at high speed when playing back taped programmes on a VCR. According to some experts, however, "zapping" at least may not result in a loss of viewer exposure to an advertising break, because the person doing the recording has to watch the advertisements carefully in order to know when to pause and when to start recording again (Feldman, 1986).

Avoidance of advertisements is not a new phenomenon. Observational evidence has revealed that viewers may often leave the room or temporarily cease paying attention to the screen when there is an advertising break (Svennevig, 1987; Svennevig and Wynberg, 1986). The VCR, however, gives the viewer even more options and power to avoid advertisements. Goerlich (1986) reported that the problem of "electronic avoidance" of television advertisements appears to be quite severe, at least on the evidence of the limited research data available. One Canadian survey indicated that 22 per cent of VCR buyers purchased their VCR in order to delete advertisements. And an A. C. Nielsen diary study of VCR usage in the USA for the period October – December 1985 revealed that around 72 per cent of all taped commercial programmes had the advertisements contained within them either "zapped" or "zipped" (see Goerlich, 1986).

Programmes recorded from the Independent Television channels, ITV and Channel 4, come complete with advertising breaks. To what extent do VCR users in Britain "zap" or "zip" through advertisements captured on their off-air recordings? One small survey among 100 householders in the Manchester area in England found that when video users played back self-recorded material containing advertising breaks, it was most common to fast-forward (or "zip") through them. Only 9 per cent of those surveyed admitted to viewing the advertising breaks when watching a programme recorded from ITV or Channel 4 (Kitchen, 1985). We decided to investigate this behaviour further in our survey.

We asked respondents whether they ever attempted to delete the advertisements when making personal recordings from off-air transmissions, and if so, how often. Often, self-recordings are controlled through a timer mechanism which determines the time at which the video recorder automatically switches on (and off). In this way, home video recordings can be made without the presence of the user, but, of course, the advertisements contained within or placed alongside the desired programme are recorded too. But when this happens the video user has another mechanism through which he or she can avoid watching an advertising break. By pressing the fast-forward or forward visual search buttons, advertisements can be rapidly skipped. We also asked our respondents how often they did that.

Table 3.14: "Zipping" and "zapping" through advertisements

	Eliminate advertisements when recording %	Skip advertisements when playing back %
Never	36	12
Seldom, that is, less than 25% of the time	13	7
Occasionally, that is 25% to 49% of the time	9	7
Frequently, that is 50% to 74% of the time	10	10
Usually, that is more than 75% of the time	19	54
They are all recorded without commercials	—	9
Don't know	13	1

The results presented in Table 3.14 indicate that more than one in three members of our video householders' panel claimed never to eliminate advertisements when at the same time watching and recording a programme. Conversely, one in five claimed to "zap" most of the time when present while a home recording is being made. And a total of one in three reported that they made at least some effort to cut advertisements out of their personal recordings some of the time. As to "zipping", if self-recorded programmes contained advertisements, more than half our respondents said they used the fast-forward controls to skip through the break more quickly, while another one in four claimed to do that at least some of the time.

Summary

In examining some of the basic characteristics of video behaviour, this chapter drew upon data supplied through diary records and face-to-face interviews with respondents. It is clear that VCRs are used regularly and in a variety of ways by most owners.

Practically all VCR householders in our sample said they had at some time made personal video recordings off-air. Most re-used their tapes, many kept recordings for a while and just a few indulged in library building. We will examine the latter behaviour in more detail in Chapter Five. Most respondents had rented a pre-recorded tape, but only a minority had ever bought one. Rentals were nearly always of movies. Most purchases were of movies too, though some were also of "pop videos".

Frequent rental of pre-recorded tapes was linked to certain expectations or experiences with video. Video users who claimed to enjoy watching videos with family or friends and who believed that video was a cheap and convenient substitute for going to the cinema tended to rent more tapes than users who did not hold such opinions.

Our VCR householders made an average of between three and a half and four personal recordings off-air per week during the two weeks for which they kept diary records. The average number of video playbacks each week was just over two and a half per week. Playbacks consisted predominently of self-recorded material, most of which had been made within the previous seven days. Few playbacks consisted of purchased pre-recorded tapes; most were rented.

On the evidence of self-reported or claimed video behaviours, men were more likely than women to buy and rent pre-recorded videotapes. Diary data indicated, however, that women watched, recorded and played back more off-air television broadcasts. Men do not therefore appear to have total dominance over the use of home video. The programme types most often recorded off-air were US drama series, children's programmes, UK drama serials and films/TV movies. Programme types most often played back were UK drama series, films/TV movies and UK drama serials.

There were differences in the extent to which off-air video recordings were made from different television channels. Nearly half of all recordings made by our respondents were of ITV programmes, with one in three coming from BBC1. BBC2 and Channel 4 supplied roughly equal, smaller proportions of personal recordings.

VCR households tended to replay recordings of programmes only from a limited number of programme types. Most respondents played back programmes from only one or two categories. These households showed consistent patterns of programme preferences. Video owners tend, it seems, to be selective and regular in the types of programme they choose to record and replay.

Certain times of day are more popular than others for playing back videos. Our respondents indicated that most video playbacks occurred during peak off-air viewing times during the evening. A substantial proportion of playback watching, however, occurred in the early hours of the morning.

Concern among broadcasters and advertisers about the effects of video on exposure levels to television advertisements have stemmed from the fact that VCRs give viewers both additional control over what they watch and the ability to eliminate advertising breaks either at the stage of recording or when playing back self-recorded off-air material. Our data suggested that many video users claim to eliminate advertisements while making recordings, at least some of the time and, even when advertisements are not cut out on initially recording, most respondents said they fast-forwarded through them on playback.

CHAPTER FOUR

THE SOCIAL CONTEXT OF VIDEO USE

Historically, the technologies of mass communication have, with few exceptions, been oriented to private, home consumption. Newspapers, radio, television and now the home video cassette recorder bring a mass-mediated outer world into the private sphere of family or home.

When each of the older technologies was introduced, social observers wondered how, if at all, existing cultural and social formations would be affected (see, for example, Gurevitch and Loevy, 1977. This pattern of critical concern and commentary is now being repeated in the case of VCRs. Some scholars (Baboulin, *et al.*, 1983; Gubern, 1985) have suggested, for example, that VCR use aggravates the already sedentary and non-public nature of contemporary life, encouraging an increased privatisation of leisure activities. On the other hand, these same critics also argue that VCRs might have positive consequences for family cohesion, as the VCR could provide a new focus for family interaction. Others (e.g. Gray, 1986) disagree, contending that, at least in the case of certain gender-related matters, video is likely to perpetuate sex-role segregated media use, work and leisure.

This chapter will examine some of these issues through the data collected in our survey of English video households. We pose several questions: (1) Who watches video and with whom? (2) Is the social context of video use different from that of viewing off-air television? (3) Does the social context of video use affect the kinds of materials viewed?

These questions are posed against the background of a general research tradition which has found that exposure to television often occurs in a group setting in which the content viewed and the gratifications associated with exposure are strongly conditioned by the social context of use (Lull, 1980; Webster and Wakshlag, 1983). This study represents a first step toward exploring whether those generalisations apply to home video.

Who watches?

To examine the social context of TV viewing and video playback, respondents were asked to indicate for each programme viewed, whether they watched it alone or in the company of other adults or children either from the same household or who were visitors. From this information, 16 social context measures were created which consisted of viewing alone plus 15 permutations of viewing with other people. The percentages of off-air programmes and video playbacks watched in each context are shown in Table 4.1 and graphed in Figures 4.1 and 4.2. These results indicate certain differences between the social contexts of TV viewing and video viewing.

Most off-air viewing is done in the company of other adults from the same household only, followed by viewing alone, followed in turn by viewing with adults and children from the same household. Relatively little TV viewing was reportedly done in the presence of visitors. In the

Table 4.1: Social context of TV viewing and video playback

Social context	Video Playback %	Off-air TV %
Viewed alone	59	25
Viewed with adult(s) from same household	22	42
Viewed with child(ren) from same household	6	9
Viewed with adult(s) and child(ren) from same household	6	17
Viewed with adult visitor(s) only	1	1
Viewed with adult(s) from same household and adult visitor(s)	1	2
Viewed with child(ren) from same household and adult visitor(s)	0	1
Viewed with adult(s) and child(ren) from same household and adult visitor(s)	1	2
Viewed with child(ren) from same household and child visitor(s)	1	1
Viewed with adult(s) and child(ren) from same household and child visitor(s)	1	0
Viewed with child(ren) from same household and adult and child visitor(s)	1	0
Viewed with adult(s) and child(ren) from same household and adult and child visitor(s)	1	0

Note: Playback and TV viewing per centages are averaged over two weeks

FIGURE 4.1 Social context of video playback

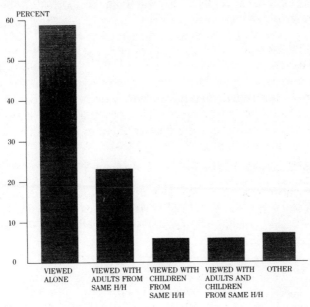

NOTE: PLAYBACK AVERAGED OVER TWO WEEKS

FIGURE 4.2 Social context of television viewing

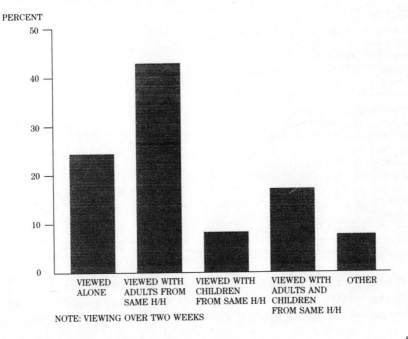

NOTE: VIEWING OVER TWO WEEKS

case of video playback, however, most viewing was done alone, followed by watching with other adults from the same household. Relatively little video viewing took place with children.

There were clear differences in the social context of video playback and off-air TV viewing in households depending whether they contained children (see Table 4.2). Compared to adults living in households with children, adults in childless households were twice as likely to view off-air broadcasts and video playbacks with another adult from the same household. Understandably, in homes with children, a good deal more viewing was done in the presence of youngsters.

Table 4.2: Social context of TV viewing and video playback

Social Context	Video Playback		Off-air TV	
	Without Children %	With Children %	Without Children %	With Children %
Viewed alone	62	58	25	23
Viewed with adult(s) from same household	34	16	67	30
Viewed with child(ren) from same household	0	9	0	15
Viewed with adult(s) and child(ren) from same household	0	8	0	24
Viewed with adult visitor(s) only	1	1	4	1
Viewed with adult(s) from same household and adult visitor(s)	1	2	4	1
Viewed with child(ren) from same household and adult visitor(s)	0	0	0	1
Viewed with adult(s) and child(ren) from same household and adult visitor(s)	0	1	0	2
Viewed with child(ren) from same household and child visitor(s)	0	1	0	1
Viewed with adult(s) and child(ren) from same household and child visitor(s)	0	1	0	1
Viewed with child(ren) from same household and adult and child visitor(s)	0	1	0	0
Viewed with adult(s) and child(ren) from same household and adult and child visitor(s)	1	2	0	1

Note: Percentages averaged over two weeks.

Finally, what types of programmes did video householders play back in different social contexts? Was there any tendency to play back more of one type of programme when viewing alone than when viewing with

Table 4.3: Social context and type of video playback

Programme Type	Viewed alone	Viewed with adult(s) from same household	*Viewing Situation* Viewed with child(ren) from same household	Viewed with adult(s) and child(ren) from same household	Viewed with adult visitor(s) only	Viewed with adult(s) from same household and adult visitor(s)
	%	%	%	%	%	%
UK-drama series	15	15	10	15	16	13
UK-drama serials	12	12	13	14	13	10
US-drama series	8	8	9	10	4	9
US-drama serials	10	10	10	10	2	8
Film/TV movies	14	13	13	10	15	17
Music and variety	5	5	3	5	11	6
Situation comedy	8	10	5	7	10	8
Quiz & game shows	4	5	4	4	3	3
Chat shows	5	4	4	3	3	3
News	1	1	1	0	0	1
Sport	3	3	7	6	7	9
Documentaries	7	6	6	5	9	8
Serious music/arts	1	1	1	1	0	1
Children's TV	7	7	15	10	7	4

Note: Percentages are averaged over two weeks

41

other people? What difference did the presence of children make to the kinds of programmes played back? Table 4.3 shows the percentages of total playback materials taken up by each of the 14 programme types when viewing alone or in the company of others.

When viewing alone, the most popular playback material consisted of UK drama series and serials and films or TV movies. When viewing with adults from the same household, the most played-back programmes showed little variation from those watched when viewing alone. In addition to UK drama and movies, however, American drama material and situation comedy programmes featured fairly prominently. When viewing with children from the same household, films and UK drama were commonly played back. Most popular of all, however, were children's programmes. When viewing with adult visitors, films and UK drama were top of the list. When child visitors were present, children's programmes were far and away the most played-back materials, occupying one in four of all recorded programming replayed.

Social context and video watching across the day

In the last chapter we reported that our VCR householders tended to indicate watching video playbacks most often during the evening and early hours of the morning. Evening playbacks were watched more often in VCR homes without resident children, while video viewing after midnight occurred relatively more frequently among VCR households with children. We decided to look further at the social context of video playback viewing across the day. For all playbacks, respondents indicated whether they watched alone or with others either from the same household or with visitors to the household. From this information we were able to compute the extent to which video playbacks were watched alone or with others at different times of day. Tables 4.4 and 4.5 show results for all households or for households with children respectively.

Across all households, most video playbacks were viewed alone, regardless of time of day. Viewing with only another adult from the same household occurred most often in the late evening or early hours of the morning. Viewing videos with another child from the same household was most likely to occur in the morning or during the afternoon.

Among households with children, once again most viewing of video playbacks was done alone. There was understandably a greater proportion of viewing done with children at certain times of the day. Viewing with only adults from the same household still occurred very late at night or in the early hours after midnight. Viewing only with children from the same household occurred in the morning or afternoon, while viewing of video playbacks by the whole family occurred in the evening. There was

Table 4.4: Social context of video watching at different times of day: all VCR households

	1am-6am %	6am-9am %	9am-12.50pm %	12.50pm-5.50pm %	5.50pm-9pm %	9pm-1am %
Viewed alone	59	0	62	65	58	56
Viewed with adult(s) from same household	24	0	4	16	17	24
Viewed with child(ren) from same household	3	0	10	8	6	5
Viewed with adult(s) and child(ren) from same household	6	0	9	1	7	7
Viewed with adult visitor(s) only	1	0	1	2	1	1
Viewed with adult(s) from same household and adult visitors	3	0	1	2	4	1
Other	4	0	13	6	7	6

also a marked proportion of viewing done after midnight with both adults and children from the same household.

Table 4.5: Social context of video watching at different times of day: households with children

	1am-6am %	6am-9am %	9am-12.50pm %	12.50pm-5.50pm %	5.50pm-9pm %	9pm-1am %
Viewed alone	57	0	66	51	57	54
Viewed with adult(s) from same household	20	0	6	13	10	18
Viewed with child(ren) from same household	4	0	18	11	8	7
Viewed with adult(s) and child(ren) from same household	9	0	2	6	9	10
Viewed with adult visitor(s) only	1	0	2	1	1	1
Viewed with adult(s) from same household and adult visitors	3	0	0	1	5	3
Other	6	0	6	17	10	7

Summary

Judging from the evidence presented here, the home video cassette recorder is a technology whose use is most commonly associated with individualistic or dyadic consumption of mass media materials by adults. Even more so than exposure to off-air television, VCR use occurs in a social context that appears to be one of individualised media exposure, a kind of communications separateness, a privatised media experience, often unshared even between members of the same household.

Indeed, although VCR users are quick to endorse the idea that the VCR is an enjoyable way for family and friends to spend time together, our findings suggest that VCR use is *unlikely* to increase the quantity of time spent with others. Simply put, most VCR use is neither with one's spouse, children nor friends.

This pattern does vary somewhat depending on the time of day when videos are played back. Hence, notable slices of video viewing are done with other adults from the same household late at night, and with children during the day.

Of course, sometimes videos are watched in a social setting. Our research as well as that especially focused on video consumption by adolescents (Johnsson-Smaragdi and Roe, 1986) has amply demonstrated a socially facilitating component of VCR use. That the findings here generally point to a more individualistic mode of VCR consumption must therefore be somewhat tempered. Indeed, future research should probe more fully the differential motivations for and gratifications associated with VCR use in different social contexts, whether, in short, the quality of social life is affected by video.

CHAPTER FIVE

HOME VIDEO LIBRARY BUILDING

Video recorders give VCR users the opportunity to re-schedule television transmissions to suit themselves. Having a home video releases its owner from the restriction of watching television programmes at the time they are broadcast. Thus home video gives television viewers a degree of control over television output unknown prior to the video era. Most VCR usage is devoted to this "time-shifting" purpose. Programmes are recorded and can be played back at a convenient later time. Video tapes can be re-used; and often the recording of one programme will not be kept for very long, because the tape will be needed to record a different programme.

There is evidence, however, that not all self-recorded programmes meet this fate. Some tapes may be kept indefinitely in a home "video library" and are available to be viewed more than once. Home video tape libraries may also include pre-recorded cassettes which have been purchased or perhaps received as gifts. These days, an increasingly wide range of pre-recorded motion pictures and episodes of television series is available to consumers in regular department stores as well as specialist video shops.

On examining diary survey data of home video use among a small random sub-sample of VCR households in 15 metropolitan areas throughout the USA, Levy and Fink (1984) found that the largest proportion of initial replays occurred very shortly after the recordings were made. This was especially the case with daily and weekly programmes. However, one-shot programmes (e.g. specials, historic events) tended to be less often associated with fairly immediate playback, and this suggested that these programmes were the ones most likely to be kept in home video libraries.

This long-term storage of video recordings can provide a stockpile from which to draw at any time. And in some households it may provide a supply of entertainment to fill in those gaps when nothing with any real appeal is being offered by available television channels. The extent to which home video libraries exist among video households, how they are used, and how they are related to patterns of television viewing and other video use, are topics to which we turn now.

Home video "libraries"

Respondents in our survey were asked how many video cassettes their household currently owned in each of the following four categories:

	Sample Median
* Blank cassettes	3
* With programme recorded off air	5
* Made with home video camera	<1
* Pre-recorded, purchased	2

The number of *non-blank* cassettes for each household was summed to produce an overall measure of the households video library holdings. One-twelfth (8.5 per cent) of all households sampled had "libraried" no tapes. Some 15.4 per cent had either one or two such tapes, while another 27.8 per cent had between three and five. Some 23.4 per cent had from six to nine tapes and 7.8 per cent held ten to one dozen. Some 10.1 per cent had from 13 to 18 tapes, while about 7 per cent of the sample had more than 19 tapes in their home video library.

In these home video libraries, the most frequently purchased tapes (60.2 per cent) were of motion pictures. Almost one-quarter (23.3 per cent) of all pre-recorded tapes bought were rock videos, while 2.9 per cent were "educational" or "how-to-do-it" tapes and the remainder were miscellaneous.

The number of non-blank tapes in any one household library appeared not to be related to respondent age, sex, marital status, the presence of children in the household, or whether the household owned or rented its VCR. However, the number of tapes in the household library was significantly related to:

* respondent social class – AB levels had larger libraries
* having a home computer – owners had more tapes
* how long had VCR library size increased with time
* believing self lacks time to replay recordings
* purchasing a VCR *especially* to make recordings
* believing VCR gives control over viewing schedule

Characteristic use of tapes

In the second questionnaire interview conducted after completion of two week viewing and recording diary-keeping, respondents were asked to indicate how they typically use their videotapes. Did they usually wipe or tape-over self-recorded programmes (regardless of whether or not they played these programmes back) so that tapes were quickly re-used? Or did they more often save these recordings in a home library?

We identified three types of users: (1) those who wipe tapes quickly and re-use them; (2) those who keep recordings for a while before using the tapes again; and (3) those who keep tapes for a library.

Most respondents (54 per cent) usually wiped tapes and re-used them. A substantial proportion (41 per cent) held on to self-recordings for a while before erasing them, with just a few (5 per cent) usually keeping tapes for a long-term library.

Differences in type of use by sex and class were small, but age did seem to make a difference. Younger people, aged under 44, were most likely of all to wipe and quickly re-use tapes. And although this style of usage was

FIGURE 5.1 Characteristic use of self-recorded tapes

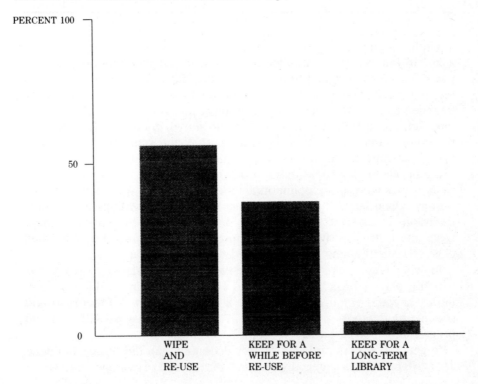

widespread among older groups too, the 45–54s tended more often to keep tapes for a while before re-use and the over 65s were the most likely library builders.

Table 5.1: Demographic differences in characteristic tape use

		Characteristic Use of Tapes		
		Wipe	Keep a while	Keep for a library
		%	%	%
Sex:	Male	53	43	4
	Female	56	38	6
Age:	16-24	60	34	6
	25-34	56	39	5
	35-44	58	39	3
	45-54	41	53	6
	55-64	52	45	3
	65+	50	37	13
Class:	AB	58	34	8
	C1	52	40	8
	C2	54	44	2
	DE	57	39	4

While keeping a diary of viewing and recording, respondents were also asked to indicate their intended use of any off-air video recordings they made. This was designed to ascertain if they intended to play back each recording fairly soon so that the tape could be used again, or if they intended to keep the recording indefinitely in a home video library. One interesting question was how well their stated intentions for personal recordings tallied with other information they had supplied about typical use of tapes in the second interview questionnaire.

Intentions to play back self-recorded material fairly quickly and then to re-use tapes were more common among respondents who said that they usually wiped tapes than among those who kept recordings for a while. Intentions to save rather than to play back self-recordings straight away were more frequently indicated among respondents who said they characteristically kept tapes back in home video libraries.

In what ways were characteristics of tape use related to what was actually played back? We examined this question by looking at how library-keepers compared with wipers in numbers of self-recorded and pre-recorded tapes play-back and, in terms of types of self-recorded programmes played back.

In general, wipers replayed more videotapes than did library builders. This difference was especially clearcut with regard to average numbers of

Table 5.2: Characteristic tape use and intended use of self recordings*

| | Characteristic Use of Tapes | | |
	Wipe	Keep a while	Keep for a library
Week One: Intended use of recording			
Playback this week, then erase	3.31	2.72	2.45
Playback this week, then save	0.28	0.26	0.25
Not playback this week, save	0.14	0.15	0.30
Not certain	0.55	0.70	0.40
Week Two: Intended use of recording			
Playback this week, then erase	3.05	2.37	1.80
Playback this week, then save	0.08	0.20	0.05
Not playback this week, save	0.11	0.10	0.20
Not certain	0.25	0.30	0.25

* Note: Average numbers of recordings

self-recorded programmes played back. Wipers tended also to hire more pre-recorded tapes, though they did not buy more pre-recorded cassettes than library-builders. Pre-recorded tapes were most popular of all among individuals who kept tapes for a while before re-using them.

Table 5.3: Characteristic tape use and type of playback*

| | Characteristic Use of Tapes | | |
	Wipe	Keep a while	Keep for a library
Week One			
Total video playbacks	3.04	2.73	2.60
Self-recorded (total)	2.56	2.22	2.30
Self-recorded (<7 days)	2.32	1.98	1.95
Self-recorded (7+ days)	0.24	0.24	0.35
Pre-recorded (total)	0.48	0.51	0.30
Pre-recorded (bought)	0.06	0.01	0.10
Pre-recorded (hired)	0.42	0.51	0.20
Week Two			
Total Video playbacks	2.33	2.25	1.60
Self-recorded (total)	2.01	1.72	1.30
Self-recorded (<7 days)	1.90	1.56	1.25
Self-recorded (7+ days)	0.10	0.16	0.05
Pre-recorded (total)	0.32	0.53	0.30
Pre-recorded (bought)	0.02	0.02	0.00
Pre-recorded (hired)	0.30	0.51	0.30

* Note: Average numbers of playbacks

How did wipers and library builders compare in types of programmes recorded off-air? Averaging over the two survey weeks a number of differences emerged. Wipers tended to record more UK drama serials, non-UK-drama series, feature films/TV movies, sport, documentaries/ magazines and children's programmes; while library builders recorded more TV programmes generally, including somewhat inexplicably, more game shows.

Table 5.4: Characteristic tape use and types of programmes recorded off-air*

	Characteristic Use of Tapes		
	Wipe	Keep a a while	Keep for a library
	%	%	%
Type of off-air recording			
UK drama series	7	7	11
UK drama serials	12	9	12
Non-UK drama series	14	15	10
Non-UK drama serials	7	6	11
Feature films/TV movies	11	11	10
Variety and music	7	7	7
Situation comedies	7	8	10
Game shows	3	5	10
Other light entertainment	2	2	3
News and current affairs	2	5	6
Sport	4	4	1
Documentaries/magazines	10	9	5
Serious music and arts	4	1	1
Children's programmes	10	11	3

* Note: Averaged over two weeks.

A further comparison was made between wipers and library-builders on types of programmes played back on video (see Table 5.5). The differences here were not always as pronounced as they were for self-recordings. Wipers played back sports, documentaries/magazines and children's programmes more often than did library-builders; but differences for playbacks of UK drama serials, non-UK drama series and feature films/TV movies were not as great as levels of self-recordings for these programmes might have led one to expect.

Given that wipers play back self-recorded materials fairly quickly, the differences between levels of recording and playback for some programme types, most notably UK drama serials, non-UK drama series and feature films/TV movies, suggest that these people record a good deal more than they ever get round to viewing.

Table 5.5: Characteristic tape use and types of programmes played back

| | Characteristic Use of Tapes | | |
| | Wipe | Keep a a while | Keep for a library |
	%	%	%
Type of video playbacks			
UK drama series	15	18	18
UK drama serials	14	10	18
Non-UK drama series	6	9	4
Non-UK drama serials	10	9	15
Feature films/TV movies	13	17	15
Variety and music	5	5	8
Situation comedies	9	9	9
Game shows	4	4	8
Other light entertainment	5	0	0
Sport	4	3	0
Documentaries/magazines	8	5	3
Serious music and arts	0	1	0
Children's programmes	7	10	2

* Note: Averaged over two weeks.

Summary

In this chapter we examined evidence for the building of home video tape libraries. Fewer than one in ten of our VCR householders had kept back no taped programmes. Roughly four out of ten had up to five non-blank tapes, one in four had between six and nine, while a similar proportion had more than ten such tapes. Libraries tended to include movies – especially if the tapes were purchased pre-recordings – and a wide variety of television broadcasts.

We divided respondents into three types according to their characteristic use of video recordings: those who wiped tapes and re-used them fairly quickly, those who held on to them for a while before erasing them, and those who kept tapes in a home video library. More than half of respondents were included in the first category, about four out of ten in the second, and just one in twenty in the third.

The way respondents described themselves, that is either as wipers or library builders, was reinforced by their intentions towards actual recordings they made. Wipers were more likely than library builders to say they intended to play back and erase self-recorded programmes within a week or so, but were less likely to say they intended to save self-recordings for playback at some time in the more distant future. Wipers tended to play back more videotapes than did library builders. There were also some differences in the types of programmes recorded and replayed by these two types of video users. Wipers tended to record more UK drama series, non-UK drama serials, sport, documentaries/magazines and children's programmes. On playbacks, wipers replayed sport, documentaries/magazines and children's programmes more often than library builders, while differences on other programme types were not as great.

CHAPTER SIX

NOVELTY EFFECTS AND VIDEO USE

Home video is a new phenomenon. As we saw in Chapter Two, we can trace its growth as a popular television accessory in British households from 1980 onwards. Throughout the early 1980s the rate of VCR penetration accelerated steadily such that it has now become the exception rather than the rule *not* to have a VCR among family households with children.

At the time of this survey, there was every likelihood that a considerable proportion of householders interviewed would have had a VCR for two years or more. While one can expect to see changes in normal viewing habits in the short-term, soon after initially acquiring home video equipment, how would the passage of time affect the way this new technology was used?

Research in the United States has indicated that the nature of VCR usage does change with length of ownership. Montesano (1986) reported an inverse relationship between length of ownership and likelihood of purchasing or renting a tape: as length of ownership increased, renting and purchasing decreased. Eighty-four per cent of new owners of six months or less, had rented pre-recorded tapes during the previous six months, as compared with two-thirds of owners for two years or more. Seven out of ten new owners rented at least one tape per week compared to about 50 per cent of longer-term owners.

In this chapter we consider how attitudes towards video and the actual use of home video change with length of VCR ownership. We examine how patterns of video use, as indicated by self-reports of video tape rental and purchase and by diary records of off-air viewing, self-recording and video playback, change as a function of the length of time for which users have had a VCR.

Attitudes towards home video and length of ownership

Before we examine changes in video-related behaviour associated with how long respondents had owned a VCR, let's look at variations in attitudes towards home video. Is there any evidence to suggest that these attitudes change as experience with home video grows and the novelty of having a VCR wears off? We gave respondents ten attitude statements which, as we have already seen in Chapter Two, can be condensed into three categories of opinion. These opinions represent video householders' perceptions of the advantages or benefits of home video, and of problems they have encountered through their experience with it.

On the basis of self-reports, we divided respondents into half a dozen length-of-ownership categories ranging from less than six months to four years or more. We then looked at the extent to which respondents within each of these divisions indicated agreement with each attitude statement. Table 6.1 presents results for those statements on which notable differences in agreement occurred as a function of reported length of VCR ownership.

As was noted earlier in this monograph watching home video is widely perceived to be an enjoyable way for families to spend some time together. To a lesser extent, our video householders also mentioned that they enjoyed watching a video with friends. Although not fully reinforced by behavioural evidence, which indicated a great deal of solitary video viewing, at a perceptual level at least home video is identified as the source of social viewing events.

However, the extent to which video householders endorse this function of home video varies with the length of time they have had a VCR. Those respondents who had video for less than six months were much more likely to say that watching tapes was an enjoyable occasion for the whole family than were respondents who had a VCR for longer periods. The trend for saying that video viewing provided an enjoyable way of spending time with friends was in the opposite direction: the newest VCR owners were least likely to endorse this function for home video. Perhaps individuals who have newly acquired a VCR wish to share it only with members of their immediate family. Later on, they may become more amenable to sharing it with a wider circle of friends.

Another important function served by home video is to give television audiences greater control over when to watch programmes broadcast by the television networks. Viewers believe they are no longer confined to original broadcast schedules, but can carry out their own scheduling to make their preferred programmes available at times which are most convenient for themselves. Home video also increases the perceived range of things to watch, serving in essence as an additional television channel. These two functions were found to apply among a large majority of video householders regardless of length of VCR ownership.

There were some significant variations, however. Respondents for whom a VCR was fairly new, though not brand new – who had owned a VCR for less than one year but more than six months – were the least likely by a substantial margin to say that compared to television (only), video offers a great choice of things to watch. Among respondents who had owned a VCR for longer periods, the extent to which this sentiment was endorsed climbed to the level observed among new VCR owners, and even exceeded it among the longest owners. Is it possible here that the initial novelty of home video creates a halo effect which soon wears off, but which returns again as lengthier experience with it enables users to

Table 6.1: Attitudes towards home video and length of ownership

	Length of VCR ownership					
	6 mo-					
	<6mo	1yr	1-2yrs	2-3yrs	3-4yrs	4+yrs
	%	%	%	%	%	%
Watching a video is often an enjoyable way for my family to spend some time together	90	67	76	73	70	76
Watching a video is often an enjoyable way for me and my friends to spend some time together	30	51	43	43	41	47
Compared to TV, video gives me a greater choice over *when* I watch TV programmes, movies and things like that	90	84	87	94	100	94
Compared to TV, video gives me a greater choice of things to watch	70	58	76	70	75	85
It is often difficult for me to find the time to watch all the programmes I have taped	50	58	58	65	64	64
It is often difficult to rent the pre-recorded tapes that I really want to see	24	30	36	41	47	31
I bought a VCR especially to build a permanent collection of my favourite TV programmes and movies	20	12	5	7	13	14

Note: Aggregated percentages over those who agree strongly and agree slightly.

discover new benefits or to re-discover those they enjoyed in the early days? One of these benefits may be the ability to build home tape libraries. This is one reason why home video equipment is acquired and was endorsed most extensively in our survey by the newest VCR owners. Interest in library building apparently fades over the next year or two, before returning again after three or four years of ownership.

Home video is not without its problems. It is very useful to be able to record television programmes either to keep indefinitely or to view within the short term at a personally more convenient time, but finding that time can sometimes prove difficult. As Table 6.1 shows, it is a problem which grows over time and becomes particularly acute two or more years after acquiring a VCR. A similar pattern emerged with regard to reported difficulty in obtaining much-wanted pre-recorded tapes. After two years, it became more difficult to find desired tapes.

One explanation for these results would be that new owners are prepared to make more time available to watch self-recorded tapes, or to be more flexible about when they watch their own recordings. They may also be more motivated to go out of their way to find pre-recorded tapes they want to watch. With increased length of ownership this early enthusiasm declines, users become more critical about home video, and expect more from it.

Changes in video usage with length of ownership

Changes in claimed video usage were connected with the length of time for which respondents had a video-recorder. There was, for example, a steady and continuous growth in the per centage who claimed ever to have purchased pre-recorded video cassettes. Only one in ten new VCR owners, who had obtained their equipment within the previous six months, claimed ever to have bought a pre-recorded tape; while nearly one in three of those individuals who had owned a VCR for more than four years claimed to have done so (see Table 6.2).

Far more respondents in general claimed to have rented a pre-recorded video cassette at some time compared with the proportions who said they had bought one. The per centage who said they had ever rented increased with length of ownership, up to four years, and then began to tail off (see Table 6.2).

There may be several reasons why rentals decline. First, after high frequencies of renting pre-recorded tapes during the early years of VCR ownership, users may find it increasingly difficult to find the tapes they really want to watch. Indeed, this was one of the main sources of dissatisfaction with home video indicated by our sample. A second possibility is that VCR owners become more sophisticated over time in their ability to use their equipment for time-shift purposes. As they grow more adept at programming the tuner-timer, their confidence leads them to experiment with increasingly complex combinations of time-shift recordings: perhaps several are programmed together over a spell of several days. A third factor could be that longer owners of VCRs acquire additional gadgetry such as video cameras, and begin to use their equipment to playback home-made video movies.

Table 6.2: Changes in video usage with length of ownership

| | | 6 mo-| | | | |
| | <6mo | 1yr | 1-2yrs | 2-3yrs | 3-4yrs | 4+yrs |
	%	%	%	%	%	%
Ever purchased pre-recorded video cassette	10.0	17.9	23.2	24.1	27.6	31.1
Ever rented pre-recorded video cassette	75.0	89.6	93.9	91.8	92.1	80.3
Ever record from TV	100.0	97.0	100.0	100.0	98.7	98.4

Length of VCR ownership

FIGURE 6.1 Change in video usage with length of ownership

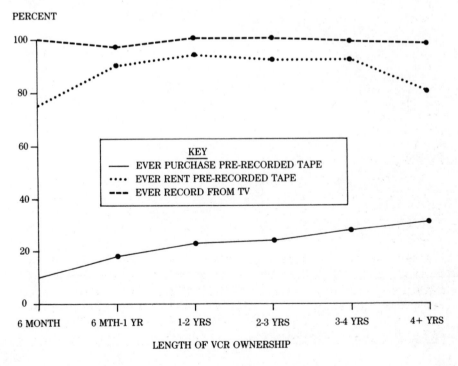

PERCENT

KEY
—— EVER PURCHASE PRE-RECORDED TAPE
···· EVER RENT PRE-RECORDED TAPE
--- EVER RECORD FROM TV

LENGTH OF VCR OWNERSHIP

Virtually all respondents, regardless of length of video ownership, reported that they had recorded programmes off-air. This is clearly the principal usage; but it is widely supplemented by video cassette rental, and over time by video cassette purchases (see also Figure 6.1).

Tape purchase

The frequency with which video householders claimed to purchase pre-recorded tapes varied as a function of length of VCR ownership/rental. New owner VCR householders were a good deal more likely to report having bought a tape within the last month than were individuals who had had their equipment for a relatively long period of time (see Table 6.3). Assuming that tape purchase follows acquisition of a VCR, it makes sense that nobody who had equipment for less than six months indicated having bought a tape outside that period. However, among householders who

Table 6.3: Levels of video purchase as a function of length of VCR ownership

		Length of VCR ownership				
		6 mo-				
	<6mo	1yr	1-2yrs	2-3yrs	3-4yrs	4+yrs
	%	%	%	%	%	%
When did you or another household member last purchase a pre-recorded tape?						
Within last month/7 days	50	34	32	22	29	20
Within last 2-5 months	50	8	23	26	10	25
6 months -1 yr ago	0	50	40	30	38	20
Longer than 1 yr	0	8	5	22	23	35
How often do you or another household member purchase pre-recorded tapes?						
Once a month plus	0	21	20	25	17	19
1-6 times a year	0	12	46	33	32	41
Less than once a year	100	67	34	42	51	40
Who generally buys most?						
Respondent	0	58	48	52	71	79
Spouse	100	17	35	26	10	16
Child	0	0	0	0	0	0
Flatmate	0	8	0	0	5	5
Other	0	0	4	7	0	0
Don't know	0	17	13	15	14	0

had had a VCR for two years, it was common not to have bought a pre-recorded tape for at least a year.

On a more direct question of how often video householders purchase pre-recorded tapes, the evidence for a difference in tape purchase by length of ownership was greater. (See Table 6.3 and Figure 6.2) Although all those who had owned a VCR for less than six months claimed to buy tapes less than once a year, this was probably a reflection of the fact that they had not yet bought many tapes. The respondent chosen in the first place as the person who knew most about the household's video usage, naturally enough claimed to be the person most often responsible for buying pre-recorded tapes in his/her household. However, this claimed responsibility became more shared with length of VCR ownership (see Table 6.3).

FIGURE 6.2 Recency of video purchase as a function of length of VCR ownership

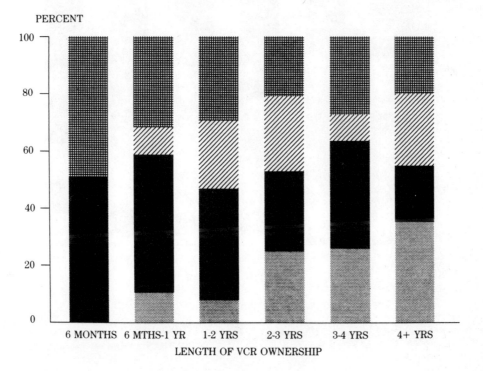

LAST PURCHASE OF PRE-RECORDED TAPE:

WITHIN LAST MONTH   6 MONTHS – 1 YEAR
WITHIN LAST 2-5 MONTHS   LONGER THAN 1 YEAR

Tape rental

Recent rental of pre-recorded tapes was most likely among video householders who had had a VCR for less than six months. These individuals were also proportionately more likely than longer owners to claim tape rental at least once a week (Table 6.4 and Figure 6.3) Among longer duration VCR owners, however, frequency of rental established a more settled pattern up to two years, then dipped, before rising again among the longest term VCR owners.

FIGURE 6.3 Recency of video rentals as a function of length of VCR ownership

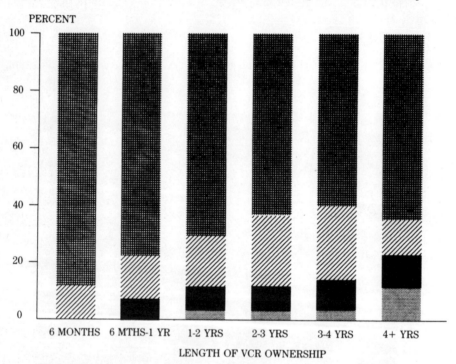

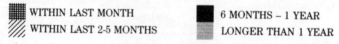

VCR rental was claimed to be handled most often by the respondent or the respondent's spouse. Sharing responsibility with one's spouse was most frequent among the newest owners and among those who had had a VCR for between two and three years (Table 6.4 and Figure 6.3).

Table 6.4: Levels of video rental as a function of length of VCR ownership

	<6mo %	6 mo-1yr %	1-2yrs %	2-3yrs %	3-4yrs %	4+yrs %
		Length of VCR ownership				
When was the last time you or another member of your household rented a pre-recorded tape?						
Within last 7 days	53	38	43	32	32	41
Within last month	34	38	28	32	29	25
2-5 months ago	13	15	16	24	26	12
6 months -1 yr ago	0	9	11	10	12	12
Longer than 1 yr	0	0	2	2	1	10
How often do you rent?						
Once a week or more	47	32	35	24	23	35
2-3 times a month	20	24	19	20	15	16
Once a month	13	26	18	22	18	12
Every 2-3 months	20	7	11	19	32	14
Once/twice a year or less	0	11	17	15	12	23
Who generally rents most?						
Respondent	40	58	56	41	57	52
Spouse	33	23	25	35	20	26
Male child	13	10	13	16	11	10
Female child	7	3	1	3	7	4
Flatmate	0	2	0	0	0	0
Other	–	3	4	4	1	4
Don't know	7	1	1	1	6	4

Patterns of viewing, recording and playback

Comparisons were also made of variations over time in off-air television viewing, recording programmes off-air and playback of tapes. We were interested not simply in overall viewing, recording and playback levels but also in the types of programmes which featured in each case. There was some indication of a profound shift in overall viewing levels for off-air television programming as a function of length of VCR ownership. However, the heaviest viewers were also the longest users. But, on balance, viewing levels tended to fluctuate with length of VCR ownership.

Increased length of VCR ownership was associated with hardly any changes in the extent to which either UK produced or non-UK drama series and serials were viewed off-air. New owners of a VCR were somewhat heavier viewers of documentaries and magazine programmes on general interest topics, while the longest duration owners tended to be the heavier viewers of children's programmes (see Table 6.5).

Table 6.5: Extent of viewing different types of programmes off-air as a function of length of VCR ownership

| | Length of VCR ownership | | | | | |
	<6mo %	6 mo-1yr %	1-2yrs %	2-3yrs %	3-4yrs %	4+yrs %
UK drama series	5	7	5	7	7	7
UK drama serials	10	12	11	11	11	10
Non-UK drama series	7	7	9	9	8	7
Non-UK drama serials	9	4	5	5	4	4
Feature films/TV movies	4	5	4	5	5	4
Variety and music	4	5	5	5	5	4
Situation comedies	7	8	8	9	9	8
Game and quiz shows	11	12	11	11	12	8
Other light entertainment	2	2	2	2	2	4
News and current affairs	19	18	19	19	15	20
Sport	5	5	4	3	4	7
Documentaries/magazines	11	8	8	8	8	8
Serious music and arts	1	0	1	1	2	1
Children's programmes	5	7	8	5	8	8

Recording levels were highest for UK and non-UK drama series and serials, feature films/TV movies, and documentaries/magazines and children's programmes. Recordings made of UK drama series, and children's programmes increased steadily as a function of length of ownership. Recording of feature films was greatest among the newest VCR owners, while recordings of documentaries/magazines and children's programmes were greatest among the longest-term VCR owners (Table 6.6).

Playbacks were greatest for UK drama series, and feature films/TV movies. In both cases, the newest UK owners were the heaviest viewers of these playback categories. Playing back of documentaries/magazines and children's programmes were prominent among householders who had had a VCR for longer than four years (Table 6.7).

Finally, we carried out 2-way contingency analyses, controlling for social class and the presence of children in the household. The general pattern of recordings and replays made over time was not affected by separate controls for either social class or the presence of children.

Table 6.6: Extent of recording different types of programmes as a function of length of VCR ownership

	Length of VCR ownership					
		6 mo-				
	<6mo	1yr	1-2yrs	2-3yrs	3-4yrs	4+yrs
	%	%	%	%	%	%
UK drama series	5	7	6	8	10	7
UK drama serials	13	10	13	11	10	9
Non-UK drama series	15	12	14	16	15	11
Non-UK drama serials	5	9	6	5	7	6
Feature films/TV movies	21	12	9	12	10	11
Variety and music	4	6	7	7	9	7
Situation comedies	3	8	10	9	7	7
Game and quiz shows	4	6	6	4	6	5
Other light entertainment	0	3	1	1	1	3
News and current affairs	3	3	4	4	3	2
Sport	3	4	5	6	1	4
Documentaries/magazines	14	10	10	9	8	12
Serious music and arts	0	0	0	0	0	0
Children's programmes	10	10	9	8	13	16

Table 6.7: Extent of playing back different types of programmes as a function of length of VCR ownership

	Length of VCR ownership					
		6 mo-				
	<6mo	1yr	1-2yrs	2-3yrs	3-4yrs	4+yrs
	%	%	%	%	%	%
UK drama series	12	10	16	17	16	11
UK drama serials	15	11	13	12	15	7
Non-UK drama series	10	5	8	7	11	7
Non-UK drama serials	12	14	8	8	11	8
Feature films/TV movies	24	18	12	16	13	14
Variety and music	2	5	4	6	4	5
Situation comedies	7	9	12	9	5	8
Game and quiz shows	5	4	5	2	5	4
Other light entertainment	3	3	5	2	4	7
News and current affairs	2	1	1	0	0	0
Sport	2	1	5	7	3	3
Documentaries/magazines	4	8	4	6	6	13
Serious music and arts	0	1	1	1	0	0
Children's programmes	2	10	6	7	9	13

Another way of breaking down playbacks is in terms of whether they consist of self-recorded material or pre-recorded tapes bought or rented from a video shop or club. Table 6.8 shows how the numbers of each type of playback during the two weeks of the survey varied among the participant householders as a function of length of VCR ownership. Self-recorded playbacks increased up to two years of VCR ownership, then dropped slightly among those who had had a VCR for two to three years, before increasing again among longest-duration owners. This pattern was particularly true of self-recordings made within the last seven days. Playbacks of recordings made longer ago were greatest among those who had had a VCR for three years or longer, while there were relatively less women among all shorter duration owners.

Playing back pre-recorded tapes (mainly of those that had been hired) was greatest among the newest VCR owners. It fell substantially among those who had had VCRs for between six months and one year, then increased to a much higher level again among one- to two-year owners, before falling away among the longest duration owners. Playbacks of purchased tapes were more common as length of VCR ownership increased.

Table 6.8: Type of playback as a function of length of VCR ownership

| | Length of VCR ownership | | | | | |
	<6mo %	6 mo-1yr %	1-2yrs %	2-3yrs %	3-4yrs %	4+yrs %
Type of playback						
Playbacks: Self-recorded	65	91	82	81	84	86
Playbacks: Pre-recorded	35	9	18	19	16	14
Self-recorded						
Last 7 days	60	82	78	73	79	74
Longer ago	5	9	4	8	5	8
Pre-recorded						
Bought	0	0	0	3	1	2
Hired	35	9	18	16	15	12

Changes in intended use of recordings over time

In Chapter 5 we looked at what VCR owners intend to do with the recordings they have made. Most keep recordings only for a short time before re-using tapes again for further recordings, while relatively few VCR users build personal tape libraries. Our results indicate, however, that these patterns vary with length of VCR ownership.

New VCR owners tended to report wiping tapes so that they could be used again far more often than did longer duration VCR owners. Householders who had acquired a VCR at least two years ago were the most likely to report keeping their recordings in personal tape libraries (Table 6.9).

In addition to reporting on their general intentions and habits in the questionnaire interview, respondents were asked to indicate in their viewing/recording diaries their intentions with regard to such recording made. Looking at proportionate breakdown of intended use of recordings by length of VCR ownership, the newest and longest VCR owners were least likely to claim they would quickly erase their recent personal recordings off-air (see Table 6.10). For the newest owners this result does not correspond with their replies to the interview questionnaire and indicates the need to treat with caution some of the claims made by those who have recently acquired home videos.

Table 6.9: Usual intended use of recordings and length of VCR ownership

| | Length of VCR ownership | | | | | |
	<6mo %	6 mo-1yr %	1-2yrs %	2-3yrs %	3-4yrs %	4+yrs %
Wipe or keep own recordings:						
Wipe	75	49	52	56	54	54
Keep a while	25	46	47	39	39	39
Keep for personal library	0	5	1	5	7	7

Table 6.10: Intended use of recordings made during the survey period as a function of length of VCR ownership

| | Length of VCR ownership | | | | | |
	<6mo %	6 mo-1yr %	1-2yrs %	2-3yrs %	3-4yrs %	4+yrs %
Intended use of recording						
Playback this week, then erase	71	80	79	81	81	72
Playback this week, then save	6	6	5	3	6	8
Not playback this week, save	6	3	2	4	4	6
Not certain	17	11	14	12	9	14

Social context

Earlier in this monograph (Chapter Four) we examined the social context of video viewing. Here we return to that issue briefly to explore how the social context of viewing varies with length of VCR ownership. Table 6.11 shows the extent to which over time our video householders watched television and video playbacks alone and with other people.

Respondents who had owned a home video for one to two years or for more than four years watched the greatest numbers of programmes off-air both alone and with adults or children from the same household. They were also the most likely of all categories to have watched video playbacks alone and with their children, and along with the newest VCR owners with adults from the same household.

Table 6.11: Social context of off-air and playback veiwing as a function of length of VCR ownership

| | Length of VCR ownership | | | | | |
	<6mo %	6 mo-1yr %	1-2yrs %	2-3yrs %	3-4yrs %	4+yrs %
Viewing Context *Off-Air*	*Number of Programmes Viewed*					
Viewed alone	5.23	5.98	8.11	7.01	6.92	9.05
Viewed with adults same house	16.40	17.61	20.08	17.71	16.65	20.24
Viewed with children same house	8.78	8.37	7.94	8.62	8.96	10.25
Viewed with adult visitors	2.68	1.36	2.77	2.12	1.12	2.07
Viewed with child visitors	1.23	0.46	0.37	0.88	0.56	1.10
Playback	*Number of Tapes Replayed*					
Viewed alone	2.63	2.04	2.80	2.44	2.70	2.71
Viewed with adults same house	1.62	1.25	1.82	1.27	1.12	1.37
Viewed with children same house	0.48	0.46	0.75	0.62	0.75	0.81
Viewed with adult visitors	0.60	0.07	0.22	0.23	0.33	0.28
Viewed with child visitors	0.05	0.05	0.10	0.16	0.11	0.12

Note: Data are averaged over two weeks

Summary

Video-related attitudes and behaviour do not remain constant with increased length of ownership; the opinions users have about home video and the way they use their VCR exhibit certain changes over time. We found that enjoyment of watching with other members of the family is most widespread among new VCR owners, while using video as an enjoyable way to spend time with friends is more common among individuals who have had a VCR longer. Belief that the VCR provides a greater choice of what to watch is prevalent among new owners, drops after the first six months to one year, but recovers again in later years. Problems with finding desired pre-recorded tapes and the lack of time to watch personal recordings seem to become more widespread as length of ownership increases.

Turning from attitudes to behaviour, reported purchase of pre-recorded tapes was greater among respondents who had had a VCR for at least one year than it was among new owners. Pre-recorded tape rental showed the opposite trend.

The types of programmes recorded at home changed in some respects with increased length of ownership. Self-recordings of feature films/TV movies declined as a function of length of VCR ownership; new owners were the heaviest recorders of these programmes by a substantial margin. New owners tended also to be the heaviest viewers of playbacks of feature films/TV movies and UK drama series.

Changes in the intended use of recordings were observed with increased length of VCR ownership. New VCR users were the most likely to report wiping and quickly re-using tapes, while longer duration owners were more likely to report building videotape libraries.

There was some evidence for changes in the social context of video viewing with length of VCR ownership. Watching playbacks alone or in the company of other adult or child members of the household was greatest among those who had owned a VCR for one to two years or for more than four years.

CHAPTER SEVEN

HOME VIDEO USE AND THE FUTURE

The future of home video

The world's first video recorder intended for home play was manufactured in Britain in the 1960s (Chittock, 1983). Known as the Telcan, this crude prototype used quarter-inch audio tape and produced fuzzy, black-and-white pictures. It never came to the marketplace. On May 20, 1974 in the Pinafore Room of the Savoy Hotel in London, Philips announced "a landmark in the history of television and the start of a revolution in home entertainment"-- the marketing of the first video recorder with a built-in tuner, timer and RF modulator (Fox, 1983). In the baker's dozen of years since, home video recorders have become common household appliances.

In this final chapter we turn our attention to the future. Will the penetration of home video continue to grow deeper following an initial, albeit brief, spell of rapid expansion? Or will the next few years witness a deceleration in that growth such that many who are likely to have a VCR already do so? Among video households, will we see changes and developments regarding the way the VCR is used? Will time-shifting behaviours decline to make way for greater use of pre-recorded materials or, with the possible acquisition of video cameras, of home-made videos? How will the use of home video in the future interact with the use of a new expanded range of television channels?

The likely future

As with any forecast of the technological future, predicting what lies ahead for home video is an exercise almost certain to produce a projection which will be proven wrong in some, perhaps significant, ways. Nevertheless, it is still worthwhile speculating about the short-term future of home video. Our focus is not with the structure and organisation of the television or motion picture industry, although obviously the strategies and marketing plans of broadcasters and film-makers do have substantial relevance for what kinds of products become available for home video use. Rather, we wish to speculate briefly on the next ten to fifteen years of home video – from the perspective of the mass media audience.

With regard to penetration, it seems probable that the rate of increased video ownership/rental will slacken, and that the total proportion of video households by the year 2000 will level off at around sixty per cent. We base this estimate principally on our findings that video households tend to be relatively young, affluent, and with children present. These three "predictors" suggest an upper limit to video penetration. Still, almost two-thirds of households having video, the VCR will be even more firmly established as part of the broadcast environment.

Developments in the use of home video

While time shifting is currently the principal use of video, it seems plausible that time-shifting behaviours will gradually decline somewhat relative to other video behaviours. In part, this decline will occur because more pre-recorded cassettes will become available, both more quickly and more cheaply than at present. Thus, an ever-broader range of motion pictures, video "magazines" and special interest tapes will compete for leisure time attention and money in video households.

In addition, with the advent of comparatively inexpensive home video cameras, some portion of total VCR-use will be devoted to making and viewing home video "movies". Whether this behaviour will expand the total amount of time that video is used, or whether home video production and viewing will come at the expense of other video or television behaviours remains to be seen. All of which is not to say that time-shifting will disappear from the behavioural repertoire of video households. Indeed, so long as off-air broadcast offerings remain at their current generally high levels of quality, viewer interest and exposure should also stay relatively high, and time-shifting is likely to remain a common, perhaps the most common, video behaviour.

Impact of video on TV viewing behaviour

Does VCR usage cause an increase or decrease in the amount of time spent watching television? And does it have a negative impact on the amount of time spent watching off-air or via cable? Bigman (1986) reported that there is evidence from a number of countries that as the available viewing options increase, so too does that amount of time people spend watching their television screens. However, TV viewing time will not increase indefinitely. At some point viewing time grows more slowly or levels off.

In the United Kingdom, self-report and behavioural data have indicated an expansion in the extent to which VCRs are used and some effect of video viewing on other television watching. One way in which the relative impact of television-based activities, such as watching video playbacks, on actual viewing of broadcasts, can be judged is through viewers' estimates of the amounts of time spent on a range of these activities. Table 7.1 shows some findings from several of the IBA's annual Attitudes to Broadcasting surveys among national UK samples (IBA, 1984-1987).

The most recent survey shown here found that four out of ten respondents claimed to spend at least four hours a day watching "live" television broadcasts. This was far more than the number who claimed to spend as much time watching video material. Nevertheless, more than one in five of all viewers claimed to watch recordings of programmes for at least one hour a day on average.

Over the past few years, however, the amounts of time people claim to spend using video have increased. Although, as Bigman (1986) indicated, there does appear to be a less rapid expansion of late compared with earlier on, as more and more people acquire VCRs.

Home video, however, is not a lone development in the expansion of available uses of the television set. In some parts of the UK during 1985, for instance, a number of new television services became available via cable. Although cable uptake in penetrated areas so far has been disappointing, in those homes which did try out the new services, viewers watched cable channels at the expense of the major broadcast channels. In research which has compared the television related behaviours of cable and non-cable homes in the same areas, the presence of VCR has been shown to make a difference to set usage (AGB Cable and Viewdata/ BARB, 1986). Altogether, respondents in the sample watched an average of 4.50 hours of television every day. The average amount of daily viewing was greater in cable homes (5.46 hours) than in non-cable homes (4.32 hours). Viewing was heaviest of all in cable homes with VCRs (5.55 hours). Both the presence of VCRs and of cable television added to the amount of television people watched. VCR usage was slightly greater in non-cable homes (0.55 hours daily) than in cable homes (0.51 hours), however. This may indicate a tendency for one service to give way partly to another, where a number of different channels (Broadcast, cable, video) are available in the same household. It may also indicate that,

71

Table 7.1: Distribution of TV use

Hours spent per average day:	Watching Live Broadcasts				Watching Recorded Broadcasts				Watching Hired video Material				Using Games/Home Computers			
	'83 %	'84 %	'85 %	'86 %	'83 %	'84 %	'85 %	'86 %	'83 %	'84 %	'85 %	'86 %	'83 %	'84 %	'85 %	'86 %
4 or more	41	49	42	40	2	1	1	1	2	1	1	1	0	0	0	0
2 – 4	40	37	41	36	5	7	2	5	4	5	4	3	3	0	0	0
1 – 2	14	11	12	19	7	12	20	16	4	5	5	8	0	1	2	0
Less than 1	5	3	5	4	8	12	12	17	10	16	13	15	2	3	4	3
Never use/don't know	0	0	0	1	78	69	65	61	80	73	77	73	95	96	94	97

(Note: Video games and home computers refer specifically to those which require the use of a television set as a monitor)

Source: IBA, 1984-1987.

while viewers are prepared to allow the amount of time they watch television to accommodate an expansion in available channels, this growth in viewing is not unlimited.

Audience research in the UK indicates that the presence of a VCR in cable homes reduces the share of viewing time occupied by cable channels, as well as vice versa. But VCR usage data from cable households also reveals that a great deal of video use is devoted to time-shift recording of cable television programmes, particularly from film channels (AGB Cable and Viewdata/BARB, 1986). Television viewing in family households with cable and video was greater when there were young children around. Cable subscribing households with children aged up to nine years which had VCRs watched 5.58 hours of television daily compared with an average of 5.35 hours for all cable plus video homes. Cable channels attained a greater share of total television viewing time in households with children aged up to nine years (50 per cent) compared with cable households generally (40 per cent). The presence of video in cable homes with young children, however, reduced cable's share (43 per cent) with then per cent of viewing time being taken up by video playback.

Home video and advertising

Industry concerns about the use of VCRs remain real, if somewhat less hysterical than a few years ago. But the truth of the matter is we simply do not know in any definitive way about either the current or long-term impact of video"zipping" and "zapping" on exposure to television commercials.

In the absence of evidence, however, we would like to speculate about one intriguing possibility, namely that video "zipping" may actually increase viewer enjoyment, recall and comprehension of commercial messages. Our logic goes like this. In order to "zip" through a commercial, the VCR user may have to be attentive to the commercial, perhaps even more attentive than he or she would have been under normal viewing circumstances.

Even while the recorded commercial is "zipping" by at several times the usual playback rate, the picture remains visible and not all-that distorted. Thus, while attending to the commercial, and perhaps being amused by its frantic movements and amounts of visual and audio information, trademarks, brand names, celebrity endorsers, and the like are still clearly identifiable, as part of the commercial message survives distortion and can be absorbed by potential consumers in the television audience.

In such a context, with perceptual guards down, the VCR user may thus prove to be an unwitting accomplice in the successful communication of advertising messages. Indeed, to the extent that advertising messages are designed with high levels of visual redundancy, simple images and jingles, it might even be possible to design "zip-proof"commercials, advertising messages which convey almost as much meaning when fast-forwarded as when viewed off-air or at normal reply speeds.

A settled pattern of video behaviour

Finally, it should be noted that like all new technologies, video too has undergone a relatively brief period in which its "uses" were being defined by the public and market-forces. However, as history shows, once common-sense notions about a new technology are formed, they tend to remain in place indefinitely. It seems most likely therefore that even though some technical improvements may be made to video (e.g. smaller, more compact home video cameras, VCRs integrated directly into the television receiver, video tape with longer recording capacities), the basic patterns of video use in the short-term are set. The VCR age has begun and it has changed forever the nature of the television audience.

REFERENCES

AGB Cable and Viewdata/BARB (1986) *The 1986 Cable Monitor.* London: AGB Cable and Viewdata Limited.

Baboulin, J., Gaudin, J., and Mallein, P. (1983) Le Magnétoscope au Quotidien: Un demi-pouce de liberté. Paris: Aubier Montaigne.

BARB (1982) The level of television viewing and the impact of VCRs. *BARB Bulletin*, London: Broadcasters Audience Research Board.

BARB (1984) Measurement of VCR use. *BARB Bulletin*, No. 4. London: Broadcasting Audience Research Board.

Barker, M. (Eds) (1984) *Video Nasties: Freedom and Censorship in the Media.* London: Pluto Press.

Barlow, G., and Hill, A. (Eds.) (1985) *Video Violence and Children* London: Hodder and Stougton.

Bigman, S. (1986) Changing media, evolving markets: New developments in electronic media from a worldwide perspective. In *Seminar on New Developments in Media Research.* ESOMAR, Helsinki, Finland, April 9 – 12, 1986.

Boyd, D., (1987) Home video diffusion and utilisation in Arabian Gulf States. *American Behavioural Scientist*, **30**, 544-555.

Buckwalter, L. (1978) *The Complete Home Video Book*. New York: Bantam.

Chittock, J. (1983) Why Britain sets the pace. *Intermedia*, **11**, (4/5), 72-73.

Communication Research Trends (1985) *Video: a media revolution?* London: Centre for the Study of Communication and Culture. Consumers Reports, (1980) *Video cassette recorders*. October, 590-594.

Cubitt, S. (1986) *Time shift: the specificity of video viewing*. Paper presented to the 1986 International Television Studies Conference, London.

Darkhow, M. (1985) Video in the Federal Republic of Germany. *EBU Review, Programmes, Administration, Law*, **35** (4), 26-28.

Feldman, R. (1986) *How VCRs are affecting television*. Paper presented at the Television Research – International Symposium, Tarrytown, N.Y., October.

Fox, B. (1983) Video cassettes – past, present and future. *Intermedia*, **11** (4/5), 18-21.

Goerlich, B. (1986) *International overview on the VCR*. Paper presented at the Television Research – International Symposium, Tarrytown, N.Y. October.

Gray, A. (1986) *Video recorders in the house: women's work and boy's toys*. Paper presented to the International Television Studies Conference, London.

Greenberg, B. and Heeter, C. (1987) VCRs and young people: the picture at 39% penetration. *American Behavioural Scientist*, **30**, 509-521.

Gubern, R. (1985) La antropotronica: neuvos modelos tecnoculturales de la sociedad mass-mediatica. In R. Rispa (Ed.) *Neuves Tecnologias en la Vida Cultural Espanola*. Madrid, FUNDESCO.

Gunter, B., and Levy, M.R. (1986) Transmission control. *The Times Educational Supplement*, April 25, p. 52.

Gurevitch, M. and Loevy, Z. (1977) The diffusion of television as an innovation. *Human Relations*, **25**, 181-197.

Harvey, M., and Rothe, J. (1986) Video cassette recorders: their impact on viewers and advertisers. *Journal of Advertising Research*, **25** (6); 19-27.

IBA (1979) *Attitudes to Broadcasting*. London: Independent Broadcasting Authority.

IBA (1987) *Attitudes to Broadcasting*. London: Independent Broadcasting Authority.

IBA (1988) *Attitudes to Broadcasting* London: Independent Broadcasting Authority. John Libbey & Company, London.

Johnsson-Smaragdi, U. and Roe, K. (1986) *Teenagers in the New Media World*. Lund Research Papers in the Sociology of Communication, Report. No.2

Kitchen, P. (1985). The effects of VCRs and remote control on behaviour during commercial breaks. *Admap*, (January), 28-33.

Levy, M.R. (1980a) Home video recorders: a user survey. *Journal of Communication*, **30**, 23-27.

Levy, M.R. (1980b) Programme playback preferences in VCR households. *Journal of Broadcasting*, **24**, 327-336.

Levy, M.R. (1983) The time-shifting use of home video recorders. *Journal of Broadcasting and Electronic Media*, **27**, 263-268.

Levy, M. R. (Forthcoming) VCR use and the concept of audience activity. *Communication Quarterly*.

Levy, M.R., and Fink, E.L. (1984) Home video recorders and the transience of television broadcasts. *Journal of Communication*, **34**, 56-71.

Liebes, T. and Katz, E. (1986) Patterns of involvement in television fiction: a comparative analysis. *European Journal of Communication*.1 (June) 151-171.

Lull, J. (1980) The social uses of television. *Human Communication Research*, 6 (Spring), 197-209.

Media Development (1985). *The video revolution* vol. xxxii, No.1, pp.1-26 Montesano, R.J. (1986) *VCRs in the USA market place*. Paper presented at the Television Research – International Symposium, Tarrytown, N.Y., October.

Morley, D. (1980) *The 'Nationwide' Audience: Structure and Decoding:* London: British Film Institute.

Morley, D. (1986) Family Television: Cultural Power and Domestic Leisure. London, Comedia.

Roe, K. (1983) The influence of video technology in adolescence. *Media Panel Report No. 27* Lund: University of Lund, Department of Sociology.

Roe, K. (1985) The Swedish moral panic over video: 1980-1984.*The NORDICOM Review of Nordic Mass Communication Research*, June 20-25.

Schoenbach, K., and Hackforth, J. (1987) Video in West German households: attitudinal and behavioural differences. *American Behavioural Scientist.* **30,** 533-543.

Svennevig, M. (1987). *The viewer viewed.* Paper presented to ESOMAR seminar on Research for Broadcasting Decision-Making, ESOMAR, Amsterdam.

Svennevig, M. and Wynberg, R. (1986). Viewing is viewing is viewing ... or is it? A broader approach to television research. Admap, (May), 267-274.

Tydeman, J. and Kelm, E. (1986) *New Media in Europe.* London: McGraw-Hill Book Company.

Webster, J. and Wakshlag, J. (1983). A theory of television programme choice. *Communication Research,* **10** (October), 430-446.

Williams, F., Phillips, R. and Lum, P. (1985) Gratifications associated with new communication technologies. In K. Rosengren, L. Wenner, and P. Palmgreen (Eds.), *Media Gratifications Research: Current Perspectives.* Beverly Hills, CA: Sage Publications.

Wober, J.M. (1985). *Screens and speakers: Ownership, use and ideas on payment for electronic devices for entertainment and information.* London: Independent Broadcasting Authority, Working Paper.

Yorke, D. and Kitchen, P. (1985) Channel flickers and video speeders. *Journal of Advertising Research,* **25** (2), 21-25.